CHANNELING THE COUNCIL OF LIGHT

MELANIE BECKLER

Swell Press

CONTENTS

"When you choose love over fear

and keep returning to love in every moment,

the way through will continue

to be made known to you."

~ The Council of Light

INTRODUCTION

Welcome! It is no mistake you are reading these words now. The Council of Light is already shining a beautiful transmission of love, light, and the energy of higher consciousness your way. Are you feeling it?

The Council of Light has something beautiful for you to experience in this book. What you are about to receive is a transmission of frequency woven into words.

Let yourself enter into a soft, relaxed state of being as you read... Allow yourself to relax and savor the message and the underlying energy contained alongside every word. Every page of this book is light encoded.

It is divinely designed to help you unlock your Divine Blueprint for awakening.

When you allow yourself to be present with the words—soaking in the energy as you read one word at a time—you will feel as if a beautiful energy of uplifting light is all around you and flowing throughout your being. *It is!*

Light and love are being broadcast your way from the Council of Light, outside of time and space, to connect with you in this very moment now.

The Council of Light is a group of ascended light beings who serve and oversee the awakening process for all of humanity.

But there's more to the story as to who they are, and I felt inspired to start off by simply asking the Council of Light to more fully explain.

"WHO IS THE COUNCIL OF LIGHT?"

Greetings from the Council of Light. We are honored to connect with you this day and to begin with clarification and a bit of a wider snapshot for you, to answer the question of who we are.

We are indeed Councils of Light. A vast array or grouping of many, many beings, all deeply and fully committed to the ascension of Gaia, Mother Earth, humanity, and you.

We serve all souls in the ascension process unfolding on Earth, both through our presence and holding the divine template for the awakening of all, and also through our specific communications with way-showers within humanity to provide specific guidance, instruction, and clarification that will most serve.

We share our message and frequency of empowerment and the light of truth that you, too, may remember your highest divine and authentic truth; and in this, we welcome you home into sovereignty and into returning to your full and complete divine embodiment.

Indeed, we are here, connecting with you in love and frequency to assist you in freeing yourself from the grip of illusion and returning to the underlying unity and oneness inherent throughout all.

Understand that we, the Council of Light, are individual beings united as one in a higher dimensional expression that is beyond what individuality can convey. We each as individuals have come into our highest truth as unique divine embodiments and, as such, came to a point of choice—the choice made was to retain a direct connection through service to Earth and humanity rather than leave and journey on.

Through this choice in alignment with the highest divine will, we have chosen to assist in your ascension process, to light the way through our unity rather than individuality. Through this, we are able to serve in a much deeper capacity, and in a higher dimensional way.

So, indeed, we are individual ascended beings who have merged our light, intention, power, and focus in a higher dimension of awareness through unity to serve, uplift, and guide all.

Yes, through unity rather than individuality we can more fully and expansively serve; for, at present, your collective beliefs as humanity are far varied. The levels of awakening have many points of differentiation. So, too, are your individual points of origin and resonance varied.

This is where our unity, as a vast array of individual ascended members, is really able to shine through in the highest service, for we are truly able to meet and greet you as one, in a way that will meet you where you are.

Wherever you are and whatever you are dealing with and going through, we have been there too.

We meet you outside of time and space, far removed from judgment. Where and how we connect with you is truly unique to you.

We meet you where we will most serve in terms of the level of your personal ascension and advancement, but also in terms of which flavor of our united expression and divine qualities will most serve you in your ascension process … in understanding and coming into a deeper resonance with your true divine nature in the present moment.

We, who embody our highest divine light, connect with you in this moment now as one, outside of time and space, with love and frequency and healing light and energy to support you in the same.

We support you in connecting with, experiencing, and embodying your highest divine light being … first as an individual, and later in unity to more deeply understand your innate connection with the One.

And so, when it would serve for our more archangelic flavor of expression to shine through, this is what is broadcast.

When it would serve for a more intergalactic flavor of teaching, embodiment, and instruction – or alternately, when it would serve for a more grounded experience upon your planet and dimension in alignment with the more well-known ascended masters of Earth – this can become our focus and perspective.

Where we meet you is dependent on what will most serve you.

And so yes, our unity and oneness – our group consciousness as you may see it – is comprised of the fully-bloomed individual members of highest mastery and divinity, which includes the archangels, seraphim, galactic, and many, many, ascended masters from both within and beyond the Earth realm ... from both within and beyond your present density and dimension.

We understand this may be challenging to grasp, for it is indeed multidimensional, and we therefore wish to clarify.

We are present with you in this very moment, now united as one within the Infinite. Through this unity, we greet you outside of time and space in the way and configuration and alignment that will most serve you.

We meet you in the ever-present now, at the point of your power to support you in entering into a new vibrational level of light … shifting, if you are willing, into a new higher timeline of possibility.

Our desire is for you to experience the profound embodiment of your highest level of divine light and authenticity, for you to embody your higher divine self, and for you to live as the fully awakened light being in physical form you came here to Earth to be.

For you to ascend, as an individual and united with all the ascended masters of Earth and beyond – united in oneness through love.

Know that we serve in alignment with the highest interest of all, according to the one True Divine Will – the one True and Infinite, Transcendent Creative Source God – which is All and which is far more vast and loving and all-expansive than you can currently comprehend.

But this, too, will become more well-known to you as you ascend and return to your unique individual expression of your highest divinity. For your individual mastery is required as a prerequisite to enter into the mastery of love in unity.

And in whatever unique flavor or shape or form our teaching and service takes, this is foundational. We serve through seeding light, joy, peace, harmony, and love.

We serve to assist humanity and earth along the ascension timelines in becoming awakened Christ lights, fully-activated individual crystalline ascended beings united as one.

We are honored to assist your ascension journey, while emphasizing that your ultimate ascension, becoming radiant Christ light and a fully awakened Divine Being is your opportunity, your birthright – to be chosen by you in the moment through embodying, vibrating, and ever ascending into greater levels of crystalline love and light.

As Divine Beings, we humbly honor, bless, and bow to the infinite Divine Being in you.

INVOCATION

Before continuing, I would like to invite you to join me in energetically centering, and consciously calling a higher quality of light and guidance in.

At this time take a relaxing breath and allow your awareness to focus on the area in the center of your chest, your heart center.

Breathe, and consciously relax your mind and your body.

Allow yourself to let go of your thoughts about the day and about whatever is happening in the world around you.

Let go and focus inward on the light and subtle quality of energy beginning to glow within your heart center.

Focus awareness on your heart center, allowing your energy to center and become fully present here and now.

Then read aloud or declare clearly in your mind:

"I now call upon Divine light, and on my personal team of guides, angels and ascended masters of the highest and most benevolent light. I call upon the love, support and guidance of the Council of Light.

Connect with me now. I ask that you support me in becoming clear and open to receive the guidance, love, and frequency here for me now.

Help me to hear what I need to hear, know what I need to know, and receive all that is meant for me that will most serve now."

Now, take a deep breath, close your eyes, focus your awareness within your heart center and begin to sense the brightest light shining above your head..

Imagine that this orb of Divine Light opens up and begins to pour down upon you, rinsing your body, mind and spirit.

Let the light pour into your heart center so that the radiance of your heart's glowing light begins to expand around you.

Allow the light to flow into your every cell. Let the light flow into your every energy center, cleansing and elevating your vibration and restoring your radiant, vibrant, luminescent self.

Breathe and energetically lift in the light. Feel the incredible light, Divine presence within and all around, that you are a part of, you are one with, and that now begins to work to empower you to realign with the truth of your authentic vibration, the full radiance of your soul power, and the Divine blueprint for your awakening to live in perfect harmony and alignment with your higher-self and your highest Divine Light.

Reconnected with the light within and all around you now, feel into the energy and love present behind the words of transmission of guidance from the Council of Light.

TAP INTO THE HEALING POWER OF ANGELS

To support your opening and attuning to the love and frequency present herein, I recommend first listening to this Free .MP3 channeled Angel Message:

www.ask-angels.com/mp3

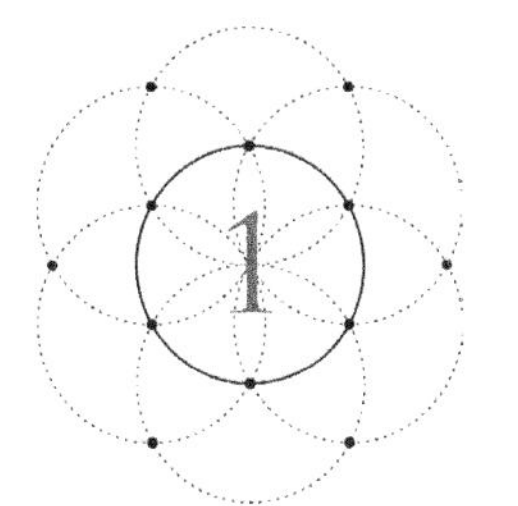

LOVE ACTIVATION

Greetings from the Council of Light.

Indeed, as you read these words, we greet you within a circle of presence. We surround you with the conscious intention to deeply attune your vibration to love.

Understand that it is the love vibration, the love energy, the love tone and frequency that creates the pathways for light to fill you.

Love creates the opening so that the light can then uplift you. This combination of love and light empowers you to ascend.

It is truly your time to step into embodying the fullness of the divine light being you authentically are, and we are honored to support you in this journey.

Know that when you bring yourself into alignment with love and light in the present, when you bring yourself and your physical being into alignment with this true power, it is then that peace, serenity, and purpose ripple out beyond you to transform humanity.

Through your divine embodiment, you as a way-shower,

pave the way for the new paradigm, for what many have called the Golden Age, which has indeed been foretold. The Golden Age is simply the full return of love and light.

Love and light are closely tied; thus, love must be carried in every moment for you to experience full activation. Yes, love is the key to remembering your true divine authentic nature.

Love is key to activating your every cell, activating your DNA, and unlocking the unique ascension codes and awakened templates that are your divine inheritance. You are now able to tap into this by focusing within, into the center of your multidimensional being, the center of your chest, your heart center.

Let your awareness focus here. And where your attention and awareness go, your energy follows. And we, through frequency and guidance, support you in illuminating your heart with love, with love in its highest possible vibration and purest form.

Let your heart center fill with the tone of love, the primordial divine sound thrusting forth into creation.

You don't necessarily need to hear this tone of divine love that fills creation, though you may. Just let your awareness enter deeper into your heart center. Let the energetic tone of love guide you, and in this moment simply allow the filling of your heart with love.

Tune into the vastness of space inside of you. Focus your

awareness on the space within, behind, and around your heart to truly experience how vast the inner chamber of your heart center really is.

Let your awareness expand from within your heart in every direction, as we now flow the specific divine tone and sound frequency of love in your direction.

It is love that heals past wounds and hurts stored therein. It is love that creates the pathway for light to then fill any holes or wounds to your heart, or even tears in your auric field. It truly is love that mends a wounded, broken, or shattered heart.

And so, this love vibration – now expanding and multiplying within you – expands out from your heart center in every direction to fill your entire physical body with love.

Breathe love into your every cell. Breathe love into every inch of your physical being. Breathe love into your physical body, your mental body, your emotional body, your auric body, your spiritual body, your light body.

This love vibration is like a magnet for the highest vibration and the highest quality of light. This love vibration, flowing within you, creates the pathway for your unique light codes to reach you.

You may now wish to simply repeat now in your mind, *I love you. I love you. I love you.*

As you mentally speak these words, really feel love for

yourself. Feel love for the present moment. Feel love and gratitude for the nonphysical support in spirit.

Feel love and gratitude for your life exactly as it is. Not as you wish it would be – exactly as it is now. Feel love, for this creates an opening in your heart center so that incredible light can now enter in.

Love has paved the pathway and now it is light that lifts you, raises your vibration, raises the quality of your energy, purifies and cleanses your energetic signature. The light shines within and around you to dissolve illusion, dissolving and removing the masks and abstractions so that in this moment, your pure soul tone can be revealed.

Listen for your soul tone now. Feel into your heart center for your soul tone. Yes, your highest level of authenticity and who you really are is represented in a divine sound, a divine vibration, a divine tone.

Your soul tone carries the codes of your highest awakening and carries the imprint of your full purpose, your greatest joy and authenticity. Your soul tone reminds you of the ways that you may most serve, thrive, love, and embody all that you are as a divine being.

Experiencing and reconnecting with your soul tone begins subtly within your heart center. Your soul tone is a flavor of love, a pitch of love, a sound of love and it vibrates out beyond you. It tones out from your heart into your entire body, bringing the love vibration of your highest truth into your every cell.

And as we explained prior, love creates the pathway for light to enter. And so, love vibrating in your every cell creates the opening for light to fill every cell.

Your being in alignment with your authentic tone means you are, too, in alignment with the highest light of the universe available to you.

You may experience the highest possible qualities of light, clear, bright, crisp, or even sparkling energy shining down upon you in every color.

In 12 colors, the 12 rays of light shine down upon you now from every direction. You may imagine this download of light as a 12-color rainbow above you with individual spotlights shining down from each band of color.

Experience the 12 rays of light each completing the circle and flowing all around you. Each light, each ray possesses a unique quality of the Divine, and the light of each ray and the corresponding Ascended Masters who oversee the light of that ray support you now in feeling complete and whole.

As each color, each ray, each divine quality surrounds you, this is more than purifying your being; this is recalibrating you and synching you with your divine soul tone.

Notice a color that stands out to you when you visualize this. Or even as you read, what specific color catches your awareness more than the others? Which color of the spectrum comes into the awareness of your heart and mind?

This ray of divine perfection is what will currently support you the most in your opening and progression.

Imagine this specific color beginning to rise in frequency, so that it is now surrounding you in an orb. An orb of colored light surrounds you in this very moment and serves by easing your tensions and burdens, allowing the activation of your highest authenticity and truth to shine through.

Let this light compress down into your heart center to receive the blessing of this Divine ray of light. As you do so, as this color heals an aspect of you, you're now able to receive the blessing of all the 12 rays of divine light into your heart center.

Visualize the 12 rays of divine light flowing in, igniting your heart light to a new level and awakening the light within you to a new degree, so that you are shining brighter, more vividly, and most importantly—you're shining in alignment with your soul tone and your divine authentic truth.

The orb of light around you now flashes to gold, silver, platinum, diamond, and rainbow light. This light orb holds the power to protect you on every level and to cut through and dissolve the layers of illusion, of density, fear, limitation, the lower levels of the ego, judgment, and over-analyzation that you are now releasing.

Release into this rainbow light, and over to the Divine.

And now, focus within your heart center once more. The love vibration of your highest authenticity is restored. The light is now able to effortlessly enter in and replenish your energy in every moment.

This is the power of choosing love. It allows the constant replenishment of light in your being.

There is a reason we say, "Choose love in every moment." And it is not for our benefit. This choice of love is required for you to fully reconnect with the light and with the highest level of divine wisdom, vitality, and to embody your highest Divine qualities.

When you choose love, as a tone, as a vibration, as a choice, as a response, as a quality, a thought, a feeling, this opens the door. It paves the pathway and opens your crystalline column, through which light can flow in.

And so, choose love.

Feel love and allow love to fill your vibration, and then imagine that infinite divine light now streams down upon you.

Light flows into your higher chakra energy centers, into your soul star chakra and into your crown, flowing down along your spinal column. The light illuminates your spine, and awakens the central ascension column of light along your spine.

Allow the light to flow down through your base, your legs and feet, all the way down to the crystalline core of Gaia.

Grounded to the earth below and the light of the infinite above you, let this column of light expand around you, opening up and allowing the divine flow of energy into your body and into your life.

Expand.

Tune into the light within your ascension column; tune into its vibrant, iridescent, warm, and truly incredible properties.

And now, tune into the space around the column that also glows with divine perfection. When you carry divine light frequency within, it automatically shines out beyond you.

Become aware of light now flowing up through the bottom of your feet, up along your spinal column, up into your brain, into your mind, into your cave of Christos, the area between your pineal and pituitary glands.

Let your mind's eye fill with light. Let your mind's eye fill with love.

Receive this activation of your clairvoyance, so you may see beyond the veil, seeing beyond illusion, seeing through fear and doubt, seeing divine love and seeing the pathways love creates for more light to enter in.

Allow your mind to fill with love and light, with the qualities of your heart.

The light of the 12 rays continues to spiral in all around you, and within you, now filling your mind, activating your pineal, and opening your mind's eye. Now, let the light continue to flow up into your crown level vortex, opening your direct link with the Divine.

Continue to lift up, up into oneness, up into coherence, up into synchronicity and rhythm with divine harmony, love, and infinite light.

Feel the expansiveness of your direct connection with the Divine. Light flows up from within the Earth through you, up into direct presence with Source. And then, the light flows down around you, creating an orb of light around you.

This is the toroidal energetic flow of your light body – light flowing up, down, and all around you while simultaneously flowing up and all around. Through the fully restored flow of light through your being in this way, your energy is balanced, your vitality is strengthened, and your highest codes of awakening are activated.

Understand that it is not we, the Council of Light, who are activating you. You are calling this energy forth through your willingness to remember how to fully embody divine love.

Remember that the more you love, the more light you access. The more you love, the higher you lift. The more you love, the more you align with your highest divine tone, your authentic soul tone.

And the more fully and completely you embody this soul tone of love, the more your gifts click into focus, the more your purpose becomes crystal clear, the more you are able to create with light and with energy ... flowing love forth in the form of intention and gratitude, magnetizing the highest potentials with love to create pathways of light that infuse your manifestations.

What it means to be a Creator Incarnate, a Creation Angel, or a Pillar of Creation, is to have the light pillar that is your ascension column at your core fully intact, and flowing with love and light. With this, you can then consciously flow love forth to pave the way for light, to pave the way for creation and to pave the way towards the golden future and era for humanity.

Your choices begin to pave the way towards the golden age of peace, love, and harmony, of each soul tone restored, playing together as one the divine symphony of love.

Feel what this divine perfection restored would be like.

Hear and listen for your soul tone and for the divine soul tone of all existence, remembering that love in the moment is how this is fully restored.

We love you and send our blessings of love your way. Receive them, cultivate love, and shine it forth. You are love and you are loved.

2 RESTORING YOUR CRYSTALLINE LIGHT

At this time, allow yourself to let go of your focus upon the external. Allow yourself to let go of whatever has happened, leading up into this exact moment in time.

Let go of what you have already read, and let go of whatever you have to do in the future. Let go, and as you read these words, allow your conscious awareness to enter inward.

Experience yourself subtly detaching from the external, detaching from the collective consciousness, letting go of what has been and entering inward to more fully meet us on the inner planes of light.

It is within the inner planes of experience that you can more fully feel and know the true love vibration, and where you are able to more fully illuminate your inner divine light being.

Know that you have the opportunity now to more fully embody your inner light and divinity than ever before. It is true. The entire multiverse is conspiring with you as you progress upon this path of becoming your highest embodied light.

To claim your highest embodied light and to fully reconnect your inner power, it takes first letting go of any attachment to what is happening in the external.

To do this, allow your conscious awareness to dive inward, focusing your awareness on your heart center.

Your unique team of guardian angels serve now to usher in the heart-healing that will most serve, awaken, and expand your heart center now. Become aware of the energy flow of your heart, your heart vortex center and the stream of heart light flowing up, flowing down, and expanding or spiraling out all around you.

As you consciously focus upon your heart, allowing your heart to open with love, you are able to receive blessings of light into your heart center, to release and dissolve old pain energy, illusions, fear, and remnants or scarring of past traumas from this lifetime or others.

Know that you are safe now in taking down the walls around your heart so that you can fully reawaken and turn on the light of your heart center.

As you take your next breath in, breathe light into your heart, focusing your attention therein, allowing the energy all around you to effortlessly flow into your heart, unlocking this sacred portal, this sacred passageway into the highest levels of divine light.

And now, cleansed and purified, elevated in vibration,

clearly illuminated, enter in.

Enter into your heart center as the archangels place four giant pillars of light around you—north, south, east, and west—creating a safe space, a foundation for your higher vibratory experience.

Become aware of these great archangelic pillars of light in each of the four directions and now arcing up above, below, and supporting you in tuning in at a deeper level within, entering inward as you are within this sacred space, vibrationally elevated, lifted up on wings of love, lifted up by the archangels working together as one, supported by your unique team of guides and guardians.

Lift up.

Your heart remains the center. Stay centered in your heart as you lift.

Tuning into a higher dimensional quality of energy that has always been present, that is always present, and that you are simply now lifting into harmonic resonance as you focus more deeply within, feel the sensation of your heart glowing and the very particles surrounding you, becoming lighter, becoming brighter, vibrating faster, spiraling around you, elevating the vibration of your present time and space to reconnect you with the experience of divine harmony and perfection outside of time and space.

Let your awareness now focus on this space around you. Expand into it. Expand outward from your heart center as you are met by an ascended being of light, a great ascended master, here to support you on your unique ascension journey.

The Seraphim who circle in around you and we, the members of the Council of Light together as one, lift you vibrationally further into an inner divine space where you are now able to experience the love, the support, and the divine qualities available to you right here and now.

Codes of awakening—frequencies of remembrance direct from divine prime Source—are now broadcast in your direction from the light of the great central sun, from your physical sun, and through the very light particles and geometric shapes and colors.

You may begin to see or experience with an inner internal sense now. Each of these sparkles of light—divine sacred geometric formations—carry the new codes written for you and for all, to embody the highest possibilities, to live in sync and alignment with the highest timeline for the new and awakened earth, for Gaia, Mother Earth to become more crystalline and fully embodying the solar christed consciousness.

You who are a part of the earth are, too, expanding to become aware of the divine perfection of your solar Christ light, the light of a thousand suns glowing in your heart center and magnetizing to you the highest possibilities of your awakening, that you might take an exponential leap in your awareness and in your expanded state of divine consciousness now.

Let your heart glow brighter than ever before, magnetizing to you now the harmonious and coherent qualities of divine perfection, bringing you into perfect coherence and harmony with your highest divine light.

Feel the sacred geometric rebalancing of your heart center.

Now, relax and allow this coherent state of love to flow out beyond you, into all corners of your life, across the planet, across the universe, across the multiverse, so that you are in this moment becoming yourself ... a power node in the awakened human heart grid upon the awakened crystalline grid of the planet, recognizing that your crystals are the perfect divine geometric representation of the higher realms of Spirit.

As you ascend and embody more of your higher dimensional truth, you, too, are becoming more crystalline in your energetic signature. And as you send out these coherent waves beyond you, as you receive and embody and shine forth your highest light, the structures around you, the opportunities and possibilities and manifestations begin to shift and change to come in alignment with this divine harmony, to come into alignment with this divine soul song of creation.

And so, feel your resonance align with your highest timeline, your crystalline authenticity, your vibrant love and radiant, authentic truth. Feel the coherent crystalline structure of divine light.

Restore the divine blueprint and template for your physical

body, so that every cell shines and vibrates in coherence, so that every organ and system, every bone and cell shines with the full light and truth of the divine crystalline being you authentically are.

Feel this realignment, this reconnection, and experience the expanded blessings your embodiment triggers around you by default.

Feel your emotional body being recalibrated and brought into a neutral, coherent, balanced state. Feel your mental body being cleansed and purified and harmonized with the divine blueprint of your highest truth.

Feel your aura and your light body shimmering with the crystalline light of divine perfection around you, shielding you from any incoherent energies and—through the consistent crystalline vibration—elevating all areas of your life, bringing all aspects of your experience into sync, harmony, and alignment with this divine crystalline blueprint for you to vibrantly live as a fully awakened divine being.

Feel your feet against the earth transferring this coherent light across the planet, anchoring and grounding the crystalline light into the higher dimensional crystalline grid and flowing forth the gifts and blessings you have to share with the human heart grid, with all of humanity, with earth and with all that is.

Know that as you now send forth willingly your blessings of love, compassion, kindness, and light towards the earth, towards humanity, towards those relationships in your life and towards yourself, you powerfully recalibrate all of these areas into the energy of the new consciousness, the energy of the awakened earth, the energy of blessing itself.

They are interwoven into your personal energetic signature, so that you naturally are blessed and aware of these blessings and you naturally bless through your being, through your action, through your intention, through your embodiment.

You may choose to now send another blessing to the earth as you vibrationally return to your physical body, anchoring the crystalline light into your body, into this present point in time.

You can, from here, step forward in an entirely new way, in a way that is in perfect alignment, harmony, and coherence with your true crystalline divine nature and with the highest expression of your inner divine light manifest in your physical experience both within and around, both in what you create and what you experience.

You are loved and supported in this process one moment and one step at a time. We are with you.

And so, it is…

3 SOUL LIGHT REJUVENATION

Indeed, we as ascended beings oversee the ascension of the collective consciousness at this time and the ascension process as a whole. We connect with you in this moment to assist you in tuning into the light, to the newest levels of ascension light and crystalline consciousness available to you now.

To receive this, let yourself begin to relax, to shift your awareness within, breathing, relaxing and letting go.

Visualize or imagine an incredible supply of divine light that is all around you. And as you now breathe in, imagine you're drawing it into every cell ... that you're not only breathing through your mouth and nose and lungs, but you're breathing into your entire being.

Each and every cell is opening and breathing in the direct divine light and presence. And so, as you breathe in through your nose, draw this light into your entire being.

And as you exhale, let go.

Let go of whatever you need to do later today. Let go of needing to focus on the external. Let go of whatever is happening in your life. Breathe in the light, lift in the light, relax in the light, and as you exhale, let go.

Let go of what is no longer yours to carry or perhaps never was. Let go of stress, tension, or emotion.

Entering inward now, focus your awareness on your heart at the center of your being. Let your heart open energetically, so that your awareness can enter in.

Focus on your heart, bringing all of your attention and all of your awareness to the point of your heart at the center of your being, this still point energy portal by which you can access the higher dimensional realms of spirit.

Tuning in now to the presence of your guardian angel, who is protecting you now and has been with you since the time of your birth—guarding your physical being, guiding you on your path and supporting you now in opening your heart wider and entering in—reach into the stillness of your inner being, into the space of your open heart, and access the zero point field of infinite consciousness, direct divine presence, and infinite light.

Become aware now of the light of the great central sun shining above you, broadcasting the fresh new codes of awakening ascension, triggering and calling forth the activation of your highest light and your true divine potential.

And as this light of the great central sun shines down upon you, imagine or visualize a golden pillar of light, a golden ray of light streaming into this present point in time, shining down upon you from above, activating along the center of your being.

Your ascension column of light unites your entire 12-chakra system of your multidimensional form in one pillar, one column of brilliant plasma light, which is being recharged now from the light of the central sun, elevating the vibration of your center, your core.

Picture this, the core of your being, receiving the most brilliant light you can imagine, so that you simultaneously feel as though you're letting go of all you are not, rising up to embody your true soul light and potential, and grounding this incredible divine presence into this present point right now.

Your heart at the center of this column of light receives this divine blessing as you glow brighter and brighter, receiving the light, the codes of awakening, the divine activation from above, from the great central sun and from the light that is all around you.

Light fills every cell. Light fills the space between your cells. Light fills your body, mind, spirit, and energy.

Supported by your guardian angel and your inner child to receive, your full soul light presence steps forward, steps down.

And now … the full wisdom, gifts, and potential; the divine brilliance, serenity and understanding; the joy, love, and harmony of your soul in all its magnificence, connects with you in this moment, aligning with your ascension column, allowing you to embody your soul light now, receiving the ascension codes and frameworks unique to you.

Your life and mission and current situation—these are downloading now directly from your soul into your body, mind, and spirit. Your soul creates a special container to receive the full extent of these downloads that will continue to align for you in the background in the days and weeks to come, guiding you in this moment to receive the perfect amount of light and consciousness and expansion.

Relax into this direct soul connection, the experience of embodiment, the "I Am" presence along your spine, in your heart, in your crown, and at your core.

And now, a multidimensional rainbow orb of light surrounds you. With every color of the rainbow in both visible and nonvisible spectrums, this rainbow surrounds you and brings you the healing, rejuvenation, replenishment, attunement, and realignment that will most serve now according to divine will on the level of your physical body.

Whatever color, energy, and frequency will most serve and heal and restore surrounds you. And on your mental body, the color that will most empower and inspire and balance flows in; as does the color that will most serve and soothe your emotional being, your energy body, your aura, light body, and your entire multidimensional being.

Receive this color, this blessing of light and healing, flowing within and around you according to divine will, guided by your soul and guardian angel to not only activate and inspire, but to heal and restore, to recalibrate and realign you with the divine template, so that you can merge with and embody more of your full soul authentic light.

This is your ascension pathway.

This is your divine light embodiment—your consciousness expanding and your energy revealing the direct link and presence of "I Am."

Feel this in your hands. Feel the divine "I Am" presence in your feet, at your root, your throat and all around you.

Tune into the space around you expanded, the vast space of infinite potential. Expand into it just for now, stepping away from the limited perception of who you are, away from obligations to experience your direct link with the infinite container for creation, the zero-point field, this vast field of space.

And now, return your awareness to your heart, finding that still point opening inside of your being. Feel your direct connection with your guardian angel, with divine "I Am," with the full brilliance of your soul light which will continue to be revealed to you.

With your next in-breath, imagine that the light is traveling upward, up into your mind's eye, your brain and your crown.

The divine light flows upward, pulling you up in vibration

and in consciousness into an embodied state of soul presence in which you are empowered through awareness of your direct connection with Divine Source and All, receiving the downloads of awakening, healing, and rejuvenation.

The light flows throughout your entire being, realigning you with your highest divine blueprint, your authentic divine template, your full soul light presence manifested in physical form.

As you now return your awareness to your physical being, feel the lightness within and around you as the full brilliance of returning to your direct soul experience continues to be revealed and continues to unfold as you shine in alignment with the full divine light that you are.

Take a moment to just feel this new energy and know how loved you really are.

And so, it is…

4 WAVES OF CRYSTALLINE LIGHT

Indeed, in this present moment, as you read these words, divine light streams in all around you. Let your awareness remain focused within while simultaneously becoming aware of these waves of light gently crashing upon the shores of your conscious awareness.

As each light wave reaches your being, imagine that it is rinsing away any tensions or pains of your past, rinsing away your focus upon the challenges of the present. Just for right now, let yourself let go of whatever has happened, whatever may happen, and whatever is happening within or around you.

Just for now, breathe and receive the direct streams, the waves of divine consciousness.

Focusing your awareness now in the center of your mind, envision your entire mind filled with light, your pineal gland being cleansed and activated with this divine light we flow in your direction.

Focus upon the light in your mind, in your pineal gland, in the center of your head. And now, tune into the space and light that is all around this center, around your body and your mind, and allow the blessings of crystalline light to flow in. Allow the crystalline light to fill the space that surrounds you, uplifting you. Allow the crystalline light to fill your mind, your brain, your pineal gland.

Receive and experience the blessings of crystalline light.

And now, focus your awareness in your throat center. Tune in to the space inside of your throat as we flow love and blessings in this direction. Let yourself, too, bless the energy of your throat center.

Let this energy untangle, unwind, unlock, and receive the crystalline downloads of pure source consciousness, crystalline light on each of the 12 rays, unlocking and opening your throat center.

Focus now on the space around your throat center and around your entire physical body, as the space around your throat receives the blessings of divine inspiration, enlightened crystalline consciousness, illumination. Tune into the vastness of the light around your throat, receiving this realignment and harmonization of your throat with divine crystalline consciousness.

Focus your awareness now upon your heart center, tuning into the spark of the great central sun you carry within. As you breathe into your heart center, imagine your breath is fanning this flame of your heart, allowing it to expand around you, attuning your sense of clear feeling, attuning your direct connection to the great central sun.

Imagine one brilliant beam of light shining directly into your heart center now, dissolving the past pains and wounds and blocks, revealing the true divine nature of your awakened heart at the center of your being.

And now, tune into the light all around your heart center, around your entire being, the light of your heart shining out beyond you with brilliant light, your heart light filling your space, illuminating the entire earth. Tune into this light all around you as this light and space around you now receives a blessing of crystalline light, a realignment and re-attunement with the highest divine nature.

Now tune into your will center just above your belly button. Once again, imagine the golden light of the Divine glowing within you, glowing within this center like the sun.

Let your will be divinely aligned.

The cords of attachments towards illusion, towards that which does not ultimately serve, divinely and effortlessly dissolve into this brilliant light of divine will. Receive a blessing of crystalline consciousness, harmony, divine will, and love.

And as you now tune into the space around this center, claim this space around you as yours to maintain according to divine will, keeping yourself surrounded and illuminated in the light of love. Send a blessing to your will center, a blessing to your solar plexus light.

Now, receive the blessings of crystalline light. Breathe and let go. Let yourself expand into the light of love that is all around you, becoming aware of your entire core now illuminated as one column of light.

And as we now increase the frequency around you, increasing the vibration of the solar crystalline consciousness within and around, imagine that this light around you is flowing into your physical body as if your skin was breathing it in, breathing the light into every cell, breathing the light into every system of your body, breathing the light into your organs, into your bones and muscles, breathing the light into every cell.

Become aware of your highest divine self stepping down and forward to turn up the dial of your frequency, of your solar light. The dial that was set to three is now turned up to 33.

Expand into this heightened level of your solar crystalline light, feeling your direct link through your heart to the great central sun, feeling your direct link through your crown to infinite divine presence, feeling your direct link through your feet to the light at the core of the earth, feeling your oneness with the infinite light all around.

Let all this light be increased in its frequency.

Let every cell be infused with divine light that is crystalline in nature, so that you now become aware of your core as liquid crystalline light, perfectly balanced, clear and harmoniously aligned with the highest light of love.

As the light of the great central sun now flows a surge of crystalline awakening upon you, let yourself—as a crystal, as a liquid crystalline light being—become fully illuminated, a pure clear channel receiving the crystalline light, receiving the divine blessings of light and rippling them out around.

Become aware of us, the Council of Light, now encircling you. From our hearts to your crystalline core, we send our blessings.

Receive.

Receive as openly and willingly as a child, restoring your divine innocence and pure joy and bliss as you receive this download of solar light, of crystalline light, of the qualities of the Divine.

The love of the divine mother is freely bestowed upon you. Your physical vessel becomes illuminated. Your space is raised in vibration.

And now, become aware of the golden christed energy of awakening that is filling your mind, filling and surrounding your pineal gland, and shining around your head in a brilliant golden halo.

Your divinely awakened aura awakens your sight, opening your inner eyes to see the beauty and clarity and divinity in every moment, receiving the light as the divine feminine being you are, creating with light as the divine masculine being you are.

Become aware of these two lights, which you may perceive as red and blue, interweaving together. They are flowing up from your very base in a divine helix of light, weaving and spiraling up, up along your core, up into your heart, throat, mind's eye, and crown.

Continuing up together, they form a chalice, a cup, together reaching up for you to receive as a fully integrated being. Recognize the awareness of your true divine nature, your masculine and feminine energy balanced, your creative potential revitalized, your clarity reestablished.

Receive the blessings of the Divine, of the crystalline light consciousness, solar christed light in through the top of your head. Feel the warmth of the golden liquid light streaming into your mind, into your throat, into your heart, into your will center, into your abdomen, into your hips, down along your legs, into your feet and hands.

And now, feel the weight of your body against the floor. Feel yourself sync into the floor, synching into the earth, all the way down into the crystalline core where you now receive the blessings of the ascended earth.

You as a divine crystalline being are completely recharged, cleansed, and purified.

And as you now bring the highest divine crystalline qualities of expression back up into your heart center, feel the presence of your divine team. Feel how loved and supported you really are.

Let your heart now blossom and open even more to receive this blessing, this transmission of crystalline love, love that is constant in its vibration, love that is coherent in its wavelength, love that is timeless, love that is clear, love that is bestowed upon you now.

Receive this blessing of love that opens your heart even more, so that on the pathway of love, greater light can fill you, restoring harmony and coherence within each and every cell, embodying your true crystalline divine nature—clear, vibrant, divine.

When you are ready, you may now return your awareness to your hands, feeling your hands filled with light. You may now return your awareness to your feet that, too, are completely illuminated. You may now open your eyes to see the crisp, clear quality of everything that surrounds you, fully feeling and knowing the true extent of the unending blessings of divine love accessed in every moment when you enter within.

We love you, we bless you. And so, it is…

5 AWAKENING SOLAR LIGHT

As we now focus our collective consciousness in your direction, we invite you to relax and allow your consciousness to expand to meet ours.

Do this by first focusing your awareness within, becoming aware of a core of light along your spinal column. This core of brilliant divine light at your center unites your chakra energy centers as one ascension column, as light.

Focus inward and feel the light, peace, and presence of the Divine within you at this moment now and let go.

Let go of your focus upon whatever is happening in your external world around you. Let go of whatever is happening at the level of the collective consciousness of your government and institutions and corporations. Let go of whatever is happening in your personal life, in your family, and the tribal consciousness.

Just for this moment now, let go, focusing all of your awareness within as your focus upon your core of light magnetizes the blessings of the infinite, blessings of the Divine, blessings of prime, Source, God, creator consciousness that stream in on the 12 rays of light into your present point in time.

Let them stream into your heart, into your core of light, expanding this light energy along your core, into your entire physical body, into every cell, into every organ and system of your body.

Breathe the light in to harmonize your endocrine system, your skeletal system, your muscular system—to harmonize, balance, and replenish the light of your mind, emotions, body, and spirit.

And now, let your awareness expand outward from your heart center to tune into the divine light and presence all around your body—the divine light, the space, the pure Source presence that surrounds you.

Expand to tune into this now.

Feel the light around your heart center, around your ankles, legs and hips, around your abdomen, around your chest, your arms and shoulders. Feel the light surrounding you like a warm blanket of bliss around your throat, your ears and head, your mind, around your entire being.

And in this moment now, let yourself expand into this divine light, tuning into four great pillars of light in each of the approximate four corners of your room—North, South, East, and West.

These pillars arc up above you like a pyramid, uniting at the center. They arc down below you, uniting at the core of the earth, creating the sacred space and container for the frequency of the Divine, of the light, of the crystalline consciousness, of plasma, to fill, to flow together, creating a sacred chamber of light for you to bask in, a high vibrational space for your frequency to rise.

Tune into your heart and the space behind your heart center as the archangels, cherubim, and seraphim enter in, now lifting up this entire chamber, now lifting you up in consciousness and frequency, lifting you up in vibration, in love.

Lift on the wings of angels. Lift into the light.

Lift through your open heart to reunite now with the full experience of Prime, Source, Creator, God, All That Is—which you are a part of and that is a part of all. Become aware of your direct link through your heart, to the center of the galaxy, to the great central sun, to your sun and to the crystalline core at the center of Gaia, Mother Earth.

Becoming aware of the orb of your light extending upward like concentric circles, expanding out with each level—with each of the higher dimensions, creating a pathway for you to travel upward into proximity, into the plasma core of the great central sun—you're still inside your special healing chamber of light and frequency.

It is now perfectly harmonized and divinely aligned, so that the energy around you infuses your entire being with your true divine nature, with your highest level of authenticity, with the clearest expression of your true divine nature.

At this point, you may receive a glimpse of your true multidimensional nature, the higher parallel, past, and future aspects of you existing along the lines of time in alternate parallel realities and dimensions.

Through viewing yourself through this lens of multidimensionality, you may recognize that every possibility is and has and will be played out. And in this sense, let yourself simply tune into the energy of acceptance, viewing yourself and your life and your path and the infinite possibilities, the infinite expressions, the infinite dimensionality that you are.

View all of this through neutrality, acceptance and love, freeing yourself from the confines of judgment, unclasping your hands from the shackles of duality, freeing your heart.

And in this moment now, call in and forth the highest divine ascension timeline for your life in this reality. Call it forth to your present body, your current life, and allow your core divine timeline to realign with you in this present now.

Tune into the light of your heart. Become aware of the feeling of your true soul desire, of what you really want to be, to have, to experience in your life. Tune in to the feeling of your every wish being granted, your every intention manifesting, your highest soul purpose aligned.

Feel the gratitude, the jubilation, the bliss and excitement, the serenity of your core ascension timeline of living as an awakened divine being in the physical on the new earth as a part of the awakened humanity.

Feel this, letting yourself release the resistance of this inspiring vision being possible, remembering that all possibilities exist in the vast multidimensional field of All That Is. And in this new energetic atmosphere you are entering into, you are truly able to call forth from the infinite.

And now, each of the Masters that make up the Council of Light, we each, from our hearts, flow our unique divine imprints of awakening your way.

Let yourself receive the downloads of inspiration, the keys to the kingdom, the codes of consciousness, activating your DNA and activating your physical body to its highest potential in the light.

Become aware of how vast your energy and light really are.

Let yourself—from your heart and from this vast powerful infinite perspective—tune into one thing you really want, what is most important for you to create, to manifest, to experience in this new cycle you're stepping into.

See the vision of your manifestation unfolding.

Feel the joy of your heart's desire realized.

What does it feel like? What does it look like? What does it sound like, smell like?

What do you now know? What do you now understand? What do you now embody?

Know that that which you seek already is so. And the more you are able to feel it and experience it now in vibration and energy, the more quickly you are able to physically and tangibly manifest this in your life.

Become aware of a symbol for this intention and manifestation fulfilled. And now, as if you are looking down at your present physical body from way above, see the symbol being placed in your heart and in your energetic field.

Finally, in a divine column of light, travel down. Return your awareness to the present point in time. Return awareness to your highest possible timeline realigned with you in the present.

Feel your hands, your fingers, your toes and feet. Feel the new level of light that has been re-anchored and realigned with you in the present.

And now, still aware of the angels and guides that are all around, receive our final surge of blessing, rejuvenation, and love. Let us recharge and replenish your energy stores, so that you are now re-inspired, re-invigorated, and empowered to play your part, to take your steps, to bring your big vision into being.

You accomplish this through action, yes, and through remaining aligned with this vibrational energy signature of being all that you are, of having that which you want.

Feel your energy now flowing down in the crystalline column of light all the way to the core of Gaia, Mother Earth. Imagine that this, your grounding column, is being cleansed and purified. Your connection to the collective consciousness is being cleansed and purified; your connection to the earth is cleansed and empowered.

Feel your oneness with the earth, with all that is, with all that you are.

You may choose to simply linger in this blissful energy for as long as you like. Or, if you are ready, return fully to your physical body cleansed, refreshed, purified, and realigned with your highest timeline, embodying your divine authentic core light.

You are loved and blessed and supported and guided in each moment. Tune in through the light of your heart. Expand to connect with the infinite power manifest through All That Is.

We love you. And so, it is…

6 BLESSINGS OF THE GREAT CENTRAL SUN

Greetings from the Council of Light …

You are, indeed, surrounded with the energy of light and divine love flowing in on the divine rays of the creator light to completely surround and uplift you, immersing you in direct divine presence.

As you now relax and let go of the focus of the external around you, you are able to journey inward, into your inner being, the inner state of your intuition, imagination, and inner light.

You are able to journey in through your heart chakra—the doorway into the Divine and spiritual realms—where you are able to access and receive a download of light, an initiation of awakening from the light of the great central sun, the central source of light on the inner planes.

And now, to prepare you for this experience, we invite you to more deeply relax, breathe, and let go. Imagine that the golden light all around you begins to fill your space from the ground up. Imagine golden light flowing upward, filling the space, surrounding your feet and continuing to rise.

Picture this golden light surrounding your legs, your knees and thighs, filling the space and filling your very body as the energy flows into every cell. As the light touches your cells, it rejuvenates and replenishes their light, restoring their natural balance, harmony, and coherence.

Relax into this as the light now flows up from your thighs into your hips and abdomen, your pelvic center, filling you with golden divine light. The light flows upward into your hands, arms, and chest, flowing in and around your shoulders, your neck, your jaw, your face.

Feel the tip of your nose relax and fill with light, your jaw likewise relaxing and receiving this divine light infusion. Relax your eyes, your ears, your entire head and your mind as the divine light now flows above your head, completely enveloping you in this energy of divine bliss, peace, love, and awakening.

Tune into the light that is all around you.

And now, dive inward, into your inner state of being, into your open heart, into the light of your heart at the center of your being, the light within you, the spark of light, the seed of the Divine that is the same light which flows throughout and makes up all.

Tune into this light of your heart, a spark of the great central sun, a spark of the infinite light available on the inner planes. Focus fully on this light. Focus your attention on this light.

Enter into this light to now sense and perceive it all around you.

The light glowing within and the light shining around now begin to vibrate faster, higher, raising the frequency within and around you to bring you into resonance.

Go inward, open your heart, and let your heart light expand.

Become aware now of four great pillars of light surrounding you in this inner realm. Pillars of light in each of the four directions arc up above and down below, creating the sacred cocoon, the sacred space for divine light to fill.

The archangels, masters of light, the seraphim, and the awakened beings on the inner planes who can most serve and support you now enter into this space, surrounding you in a great circle of light.

Become aware of this, your divine team supporting you in entering deeper within.

And as you now tune in to the light of your heart, envision it glowing brighter than before. Send a blessing to your heart. Send gratitude to your heart for its light and presence within you, for the light it shines into the world and all around. Send love.

The energy of blessing to your very heart center initiates a wave of love vibration as your heart responds and ripples out this same energy of blessing far beyond. This energy of blessing opens the doors of your heart for you now to dive deeper within, traveling deep into the inner realms.

In this inner realm of your heart, now begin to lift—lifting up on the wings of angels who lower their vibration down to meet you in this moment, lifting up on the pure divine light and presence, lifting you up on a pillar of awakening, lifting you up into the light, above the light, into direct presence and proximity with the source of all light on the inner realms—into oneness, into resonance, into coherence, into the very center of the great central sun.

Envision the light of this sun glowing brightly before you, its golden, iridescent, diamond light above, below, and all around.

And as you deeply relax now into this present experience with the light of the great central sun, let yourself become aware that you are it, that the light of your heart is one with the light of the great central sun and one with all of creation.

Feel your oneness with the light, oneness with the great central sun, oneness with all of creation, with All That Is. Let yourself expand to experience the full extent of that which you are.

Expand your inner light to fill your home. Expand your inner light to fill your state. Expand your inner solar light to fill your country. Expand your inner solar light to fill and surround the entire earth, becoming aware of all the crystals of the earth sending you their blessings.

Receive this blessing vibration and send your love and gratitude and blessing back, which raises your vibration further, so that you are now able to expand to the crystalline grid level, the fifth dimensional crystalline grid that surrounds Gaia, Mother Earth.

Tune into the light of the crystalline grid, which receives the direct downloads of the Divine and releases them to you when you are ready. Receive now the downloads of awakening, of blessing, of harmony, of initiation light and love as you now expand to the galactic level, becoming aware of your full multidimensionality, your vast inner star light that is a part of and that blesses all of existence.

At this galactic level, become aware of yourself as a star in your own right.

Your crystalline core at your center vibrates in perfect harmony and coherence, the liquid light of your core. Let it shine. Let it fill your every cell with light. Let it restore perfect balance and harmony.

Let it heal, uplift, and inspire. Let it rise to your surface and shine far beyond.

Shine your light, becoming aware now of your orbit as a star around the great central sun, this sun of inner light, of divine inspiration, the source of your power, the source of your magnificence, the source which is not separate, but is a part—or rather, you are a part of it and you are one with this great central sun and one with all.

And from your heart center, feel your direct connection with the light of the central sun.

Now, in three, two, one, receive a download, an initiation, an illumination of your heart center bringing you direct from Source the new levels of light in the fullest and most complete package which you can safely download and with which you can shine.

All that is beyond your current grasp and reach is anchored into the light of the crystalline grid of the earth. It is waiting, ready for when you are ready to lift even higher.

But for now, receive the highest level of light that is possible for you to safely and harmoniously embody. And shine with this inner light of divinity, restoring your divine blueprint and template as a being of light, as a star in the inner realms.

And as a star, feel yourself now blessing the entirety of all that is. From your heart, the center of your starlight and being, send out the light of love, sending your blessing to all of existence, to the entire galactic sphere.

Send your blessing to the entire universe.

Send your blessing to the crystalline grid.

Send your blessing to the crystals of the earth.

Send your blessing to the earth.

Send your blessing to the awakened human heart grid, blessing the collective consciousness, blessing your geographic location, blessing the city you're in, blessing your home. Now do it once again—blessing your own heart, blessing your inner core of light, blessing every cell in your physical body.

Send the blessings of the light to your mind, to your emotions.

And as you now send your blessings of love, gratitude, harmony, kindness, and compassion to the inner light itself, to the source of inner light, to the great central sun, send the energy of blessing.

And now, receive this back tenfold, opening your arms wide to receive the infinite blessing of light, harmony, love, abundance, balance from All That Is, completely illuminating your inner core of light, which now shines brighter than ever before, acting like a beacon and a magnet for the many blessings that are yet in store.

In this vibrational state, let yourself now return your awareness to that core desire, to what you really want.

What is most important for you to experience in this physical incarnation of Divine Source light manifest as you? What do you call forth from the vast realm of infinite possibility? What will you infuse with the direct light of the great central sun?

Tune into this core desire for what you want to create and have and be and experience and see as the reality of this manifestation. Feel the gratitude, the joy, the excitement of having this, of being this.

Send the energy of blessing, of light, from your heart to all of creation for bringing you your true heart's desire—blessing your future self, the full embodiment of all that you are; your past selves, who have led you to this point in time; and your present self with your heart open.

Receive now the initiation of light from the great central sun, paving the pathway of light for more of your divine higher self to be embodied through you, as you, for you to step up and step into living as the divine being in physical form you authentically are, the light being, fully awakened and illuminated, shining your light out to bless and uplift and harmonize all.

And through the very design of creation, this energy of blessing All That Is returns the blessings of the infinite to you in the present, pouring into your heart center, lifting you higher, expanding you and completely restoring your core of light.

Your access to the infinite light of the inner realms allows this inner light to be broadcast and mirrored in the external all around. The inner peace, joy, bliss, abundance you carry within naturally, as a result, manifests around.

Feel the light that is all around you, the light that you are shining, the light that fills your space above, below, beside, in front, behind.

Claim this light, this space, as your own, letting the doors of your heart remain open, letting the spark of the great central sun you carry within illuminate your surroundings, letting yourself shine as the divine light being, as the star shining the fullness of the light you authentically are.

You are loved and we now send our blessing, gratitude, peace, inspiration, and our conscious blessing your way.

Receive this and now return your awareness to your physical space, to this present point in time that has been illuminated, knowing that within you and around you is filled with the energy of the light.

Look for signs and validations of this light presence. If you're not feeling it, return to the energy of blessing.

Bless your heart to awaken your heart light.

Bless your surroundings to awaken the light that is always present all around.

We love you, we bless you. And so, it is…

7 EMBRACING THE INFINITE

Indeed, we are here, connecting with you with love and frequency to assist you in freeing yourself from the grip of illusion and return to the underlying unity and oneness inherent throughout all.

And so, at this time, let yourself relax—for it is from a relaxed perspective that you are able to feel our presence, to see the underlying divine perfection, to know your full authenticity, and to hear the wisdom of your inner being, your divine authentic truth.

Understand that when you enter inward, when you focus upon your heart center and let your heart become illuminated with light, this is not simply a fun exercise; this is not simply the only way for you to vibrationally shift.

Your heart, this energetic center, is at the center of your multidimensional being.

And so, when you detach your awareness from the external, from the lines of time, from your body and from your present point in time ... and when you fully and completely enter into the space of your heart, you enter into the heart portal that allows you infinite access to the higher realms.

You allow an elevator-type experience of ascension to elevate your perspective above the 3D realm you partake in, above the fourth dimension of your dreams and imagination, above the dimension where space and time resides.

You lift up through the light in the center of your being, through the light which fills your heart, which expands out beyond your heart center.

You welcome the warmth and glow and the sacred geometric tone of divine perfection that begins harmonizing with your every cell, bringing every cell of your physical body into this love coherence, into sync with the divine unity and oneness of creation, into the bliss, peace, and presence with the infinite, with the Divine, with the light that is all around you, that glows within you and that you are now able to sense, see, know, feel, experience, hear, and merge with.

Become the light that is within you.

As you breathe in, tune into light glowing within you. As you breathe out, tune into the light expanding around.

Let your light body merge with the infinite light of the universe, merge with the greater circle of oneness that we, the Council of Light, hold. Merge with the light, knowing that you are safe and supported in expanding, letting go of time and space and being, tuning into the void and to the divine feminine light that is the container for all existence.

Feel the space, the bliss, the harmony, peace, and light that surrounds you.

Experience the vastness of this light extending far, far beyond your body, your space, your earth. Tune into the light on a global scale and beyond. Breathe and become the light.

Return, merged with this divine presence—with this light frequency, expanding, lifting, shining, shining like a solar being, illuminated with Christ light within and around—embodying source level consciousness, the light of your sacred heart expanding outward and upward.

Now, tune into the light in the area of your throat. Tune into the light within your throat center. Breathe and become aware.

And now, tune into the light and space around your throat, receiving the blessing of love, receiving the blessing through simply tuning into your oneness with the infinite, empowering your ability to clearly hear divine love, to speak divine truth, to be fully present, one with the light that makes up all.

Now, tune in to the space at the back of your head. Between the top of your head and neck, find this point glowing with light.

Tune into the light in this space inside of your head. And now, tune into the light glowing around, expanding out far beyond, illuminating the pathway for you to experience the Divine, to experience all of the divine qualities and all of the beings of light and love who embody these divine qualities to serve you in your growth.

Open this portal to connect with your spiritual teachers and guides on the higher planes, your casual chakras. Let the light and the space around this center expand all the way out to a global level.

You are this vast. And now, receive the blessing, the unification, the purification, the divinity codes to heal, restore, activate, and elevate this center.

Now, tune into this center within your head and the vast field of consciousness which occupies the space, the light around you, the divinity within and around.

Bring your awareness now to the center of your mind, to this light and space which occupies the interior of your mind, your pineal gland illuminating with light, receiving the codes of clarity, peeling back the veil of illusion, revealing the divinity within you and all.

Tune into this light at the center of your head. And now, tune into the light expanding around, extending outward from the center of your head, out beyond your body, out beyond your present space, out beyond where it merges with the light of the Infinite, with the light of the Divine, with the space and light that is one with all.

And now, through this connection with the infinite, let your pineal gland receive a blessing and activation of the highest light. Receive the DNA and cellular upgrades available to you now as a divine being, a spiritual being in physical form.

Activate clairvoyance, lucidity, wisdom, and your direct link with the infinite found in this golden light at the center of your mind that fills your entire head, that expands out to fill your entire body with a golden light. Feel this golden light orb illuminating every cell.

Any negativity, any lower vibration, any past fear or pain or emotion cannot reside in this high frequency of the Divine. And so, all that is not divine, all that is not your authentic truth, all that is not your pure knowingness and wisdom and light, all that is not your full authenticity is released.

This golden orb of light around you shines brighter. Tune into the light around it, the light around you. Become aware of where you end and where the infinite begins, recognizing there is no border; there is no boundary line.

You are the infinite.

You are the same particle of light and facet of consciousness that makes up all. And when you expand, when you activate your pineal, when you lift and expand out beyond, you are able to feel and know and experience this oneness, light, and bliss.

Now, become aware of the space at the very top of your head glowing with golden, diamond, platinum light, rekindling the full knowingness of your oneness with source.

And as you now take a deep breath in, imagine you're pulling your energy up towards your crown chakra, this point at the top of your head and up and out of your body, into the divine light, into divine presence.

Breathe in and lift.

Expand.

Expand into the space around this center. Expand into the space above and all around you, light flowing around your entire physical being, below your feet, above your head. This orb of divine light and presence illuminates the authentic divine being you are, so that you see through illusion, claiming rather your power.

Know that in this space, in this now, in this moment, you are connected to the Divine, you are connected to your light body, you are connected to the infinite, and infinite possibility awaits you.

Anything is possible.

And so, choose to flow this energy towards what you really want, towards the future you want to create, choosing to consciously call back worries and thoughts and doubts about the future, choosing to stop repeating the emotions which are only memories tied to the past.

Be present in the moment, knowing that in this point in time, in this space, in this vast energy you have expanded into, you cannot only know your highest path, you cannot only catch a glimpse of all that is possible for you, but you can step into it and embody it and celebrate this, your divine light, your awakened divinity as a light being, sitting in the circle of oneness through embodying this higher light of all.

Through simply shining and being this magnificence, your physical vitality is restored, your mental clarity illuminated, your intuition elevated, the opportunities and potentials for your life highlighted.

Tune into the light now glowing along your spine, uniting all of the energy centers of your physical body as one pillar, one column of unity, of light, of love. This action brings the light, the love, the divinity to your every cell and cannot help but ripple out beyond you, flowing this coherent love, this divine presence out into your day, into your week, into your life, into the greater fields of consciousness, into the All.

Breathe and focus once again within your heart. Focus on the golden light of your inner sun within.

And now, let your awareness return to your body which is now entirely new, which is recharged by the Divine, by divine presence. Return to your life which is rekindled and refreshed, which is entirely new. Look for the signs of this divine connection.

Look for the new level which is now opening to you and appearing before you. Be willing to let go of the patterns of past, to let go of the known future, to let go of needing to know. Step into the unknown, for in this your highest destiny is revealed.

And when your heart is open, when your light is turned on in this way, trust that you are guided, trust that all is well, trust that the way through the unknown will appear and will carry you into the new that is more vibrant, fulfilling, and positive than you could ever imagine.

Be willing to surrender the specifics and walk the fine line, the path of light, between intention and being clear about the higher level of light you are moving into, and surrender to things happening according to Divine Will in a way that is different and even more miraculous, even more rewarding and positive and joyful than you could ever imagine.

This is the paradigm you're stepping into, of living in sync with the Divine, of living as an awakened being, trusting and loving and moving forward and allowing the universe to surprise you, to guide you, and to realign you with the highest possible expression of love.

For this is what you are. Day by day and moment by moment and during periods where you tune into increased surges of light, as you are doing now, you progress exponentially in becoming one with the full light and authenticity that you are.

You become aware and return to the profound experience of living in sync with this divine oneness and love always and all times.

We are the Council of Light. We bow to you, we honor you, we bless you as you flow this increased vibration and frequency into all corners of your world and all aspects of your life.

This is powerful light work that is blissful and joyful for you to behold.

And so, with an open heart, open mind, open ascension column of light, your toroidal fields intact, your light body illuminating, step forward into your new life that has been paved by the light of the Divine.

We love you and bless you.

And so, it is…

8 AWAKEN YOUR ANGELIC SELF

We are honored to connect with you now in this most exciting time at the precipice of your collective jump-off point, where you are able to leap into a higher level of experience as an individual and as a collective.

We connect with you to support you in this transitionary period to assuage your fears and assure you that this leap does not entail leaving anything behind other than fear, doubt, and lower vibrational altered states.

This realignment is your reconnection and merging with your authentic state, your natural state that is, indeed, oneness with "I Am" presence, with Source, God, creator source light.

Let us affirm this: your natural state is in oneness with the Divine, the illuminated, joyful, radiant, connected creator state where you align with your powers of creative manifestation and embody a high vibration, a beautiful state of bliss, joy, and light.

And the negative emotions—fear, anxiety, insecurity, impatience, frustration, and anger—are the altered states of illusion, lower vibrational fight-or-flight response.

These mechanisms of illusion place a ceiling on your growth potential and manipulate you away from your authenticity and truth.

So, change and let go of these default reactions, which are learned and triggered from a lower vibrational state of being.

This will empower you to respond in the present moment with love, to return to the observer state of nonjudgment, of divine neutrality, and step back into the natural authentic state of your higher vibrational truth—the fifth-, seventh-, and ninth-dimensional angelic creator being you authentically are.

Yet let us not just *talk* about this highest level of light, but rather assist you in making the leap and shift to embody a higher dimensional aspect of yourself. Let us assist you in connecting with your greater authenticity and brilliance right here and now.

Understand that connecting with this true creator state—this high vibrational angelic state in your meditation, contemplation, and sitting—is just the start. This leap point we speak of, this jump-off point, this transitionary period and ascension, is aligning you with your creator state, your angelic state, your divine human state as a christed being, creator man, God man, divine human being, which you embody in every moment.

This is where you are headed.

And no, this is not an exaggeration or a stretch. Your participation and intention to embody this awakened crystalline state is indeed required, as well as your willingness to observe where you are now.

By acknowledging this simple differentiation that your natural and authentic state is divine and angelic, as a divine creative being, choose to let go of the addictive emotions, patterned responses, old paradigms of experience, and peel back these altered states of consciousness, these manipulated states of being.

Reveal the essence, the divine light within you, allowing it to rise up, shine forth, and become the foundation for your new experience in living as an awakened light being on the new earth.

Indeed, the old earth is not going anywhere; it will remain. The duality paradigm is not going anywhere; it will remain. But the doors are open to you, as an individual and collectively, to enter into a new dimension of experience, the higher vibrational overlay at a new level.

Take the staircase of light into a higher dimensional experience, which has been here all along but is now accessible.

Now we invite you to let yourself relax, breathe, and settle in where you are. Find a position of comfort as you breathe, and let go of the altered states of tension, fear, and frustration. Recognize these are not yours and are not even you, but are simply constructs and layers of illusion, defensive response mechanisms, which you are safe and supported in letting go of now.

We flow a specific frequency into your time and space to assist you in releasing lower negative emotions.

At this time, let yourself focus on one habitual response, one negative emotion, one altered state and way of relating to your world that seems to be repeatedly operating. Is it anger, frustration, tension, stress, anxiety, sadness, depression, irritability, impatience?

Tune in to just one altered state that you, from time to time, still experience as your own. Tune in to and feel this. Recognize this is not yours or you.

And right now, feel it lift away, peeling back from your energetic signature like a dark window cling being peeled off a window. Increased clarity, lightness, and your authentic state can now shine forth.

Let it go and let your awareness return within.

As liquid light pours into this present point in time where you are sitting or lying, imagine it beginning to pool like water around your feet. Where it touches your feet, you feel density melt away, and they begin to tingle and glow with warmth and light.

This liquid light continues to stream in and elevates the vibration below your feet, creating a foundation of light for you to lift in. This is pure divine presence and creative energy, as the golden, platinum, iridescent light streams in around your feet.

It continues to rise like water up along your calves into your knees, your thighs, and along the full length of your legs, into your hips, waist, lower abdomen, and belly, submerging your lower half with light; then up into your waist, your hands, wrists, and arms, your chest, shoulders, and neck.

As it fills this time and space, it helps you to deeply relax. The liquid crystalline light all around you continues to rise up above your chin, mouth, nose, and ears, then above your head.

You can effortlessly breathe, but you are completely immersed in liquid crystalline light, so your body becomes weightless as if you're floating in saline water.

This liquid light rises up so the entire room and home you're in is filled, and the entire city, state, and country are filled with this light that you are effortlessly floating in, illuminated and immersed in.

As its level rises, you rise up with it, lifting and floating, relaxed, peaceful, blissful, tingling in the beautiful, iridescent, crystalline liquid light all around you, glowing brighter than the sun, filling your every cell with light, filling your aura, your light body, your mind, body, and spirit with divine light and presence.

The entire earth is immersed in this golden, diamond, platinum crystalline light of the Divine, of the awakening and love.

Lift in it and let your consciousness expand to experience yourself as not being separate from but one with the crystalline light you are immersed in, which fills the entire globe. Lift and float up in it as you deeply relax and are completely illuminated, rising in conscious awareness into direct presence with Source, God, and divine light all around you.

Lift up, way up in consciousness to experience your oneness with the Divine and all that is. Your oneness with the earth, Source, light, this high vibrational, peaceful, blissful, radiant illumination is your natural state of being.

From this place, let yourself, once again, become aware of that lower vibrational emotion or pattern you've been struggling with. Recognize its smallness, how insignificant that little emotional response is compared to your vastness and this incredible light.

In this space, you are able to observe and not become bogged down in it. Recognize it for what it is—illusion, a construct of the illusion, or an altered lower vibrational state.

Let it go.

Release it and return to your authenticity, your glowing, brilliant, illuminated self, one with Source, the Divine, and All That Is.

And in this place, your highest vibrational self, your

seventh- and ninth-dimensional angelic self steps forward, glowing pure light into your present point in time.

You may see a radiant golden light in the left side of your mind's eye as your higher self comes into view and focus, embodying a core quality of your authentic truth. Become aware of this divine quality—love, serenity, radiant bliss, presence, neutrality—that is authentically you and represents the higher vibrational pattern and response, the mirror of the lower emotion you've been struggling with.

What is the quality your higher self now draws your awareness to? What is it that your higher self serves to embody or claim as a natural state of your being? What will support you in transcending the lower levels and retaining this high vibrational state and connection?

Tune into this divine quality and feel its presence all around, as it integrates into your being and you shine this divine quality forth. Let yourself focus on your heart center glowing with divine light and presence, the flame of the Divine glowing brightly within you.

Your authentic light shines forth, glowing so brightly that it touches every cell and effortlessly expands around you in an orb, creating the most powerful shield of divine love and joy.

It is your authentic energetic signature; let yourself know, feel, and understand that this is not an altered state or a limited experience. This is something in which you are able to stay, embody, and shine forth always at all times, for this is your truth outside time and space.

And so, you are able to bring it into physical being, into the present time and space by returning to open heart awareness. The flame brightly glows within you and illuminates your entire being, so you are shining brightly.

At this point, tune into the orb of light, the golden crystalline diamond light around you.

The full presence of your angelic self, your seventh- and ninth-dimensional angelic being steps forward into your awareness, merging with you in your physical form. More of your authenticity and power, your higher light enters into your body, mind, spirit, and awareness, downloading the full presence of your highest self.

Now embody this higher vibrational self, your angelic self; lift up, expand, glow, and shine. As your angelic self steps into being, open your heart and think, *Yes.*

Let yourself expand, and let your heart light glow to strengthen this connection.

Become aware of your etheric wings reaching back around you, the etheric wings of your angelic self merging with you in this now. Feel their beauty and light, as they completely fill out with divine light and presence.

Feel yourself embodying the divine blueprint for the awakened light being, the angelic being that is your natural state of being, which you are bringing into physical form now. Embody this light and become aware of your angelic halo, the light glowing above your head.

Your crown chakra effortlessly opens to allow pure divine presence in every moment, to allow your unimpeded link to pure source, God light.

Divine light pours into your crown through your angelic halo, into your third eye, opening your sight; into your throat, opening your ability to listen, hear, and communicate; and into your heart, opening your highest sense of divine love.

As this light continues to flow down, an orb surrounds your lower chakras, your sacral, solar plexus, root, and earth chakras, protecting you with love and joy from any lower vibrational connections or cords.

Now through your upper energetic centers—your heart, throat, third eye, crown, and soul star—you can unite and link with and embody your authentic truth, your angelic self, your creator state.

Know that in this place, you as an angelic being are directly linked to Creator, God, Source through your open heart, throat, third eye, crown, and soul star.

And the pillar of light that unites all these energetic centers as one flows along the core of your physical body, directly linking you to Creator, Source above. It then flows down all around, filling out your light body, connecting you to the awakened earth, the crystalline core of Gaia below.

As it streams up, down and all around, you are united to the awakened earth, united with Creator, Source.

And in this place, in this state, in this authentic embodiment of your truth, you are invited to claim your power as creator being to cocreate with God, Source, and Light, beginning with what is a facet of your true soul purpose, not yet fully realized in physical form—abundance, connection, cocreation, service, and love.

What is this for you? Receive the feeling, the knowing of what you can, as this angelic being, cocreate with Source, God, Creator. Become aware conceptually and vibrationally, knowing in this moment you are in alignment with this creation.

Now,as you step back into the physical, you are able to retain this creator state. Yet there will be a period of practice and integration where you will have to choose through intention and action in the present moment to stay in this higher vibrational state.

If a lower emotion, a response mechanism, or the illusion response, the altered state reemerges, choose to think or say aloud: *Change or shift. I choose to change. I choose to shift.*

Reconnect with your heart light and let it open.

Step back into the perspective of observer, of your angelic self and choose to shift; elevate your vibration and realign with your angelic self.

Feel creator light pouring in through your crown into your

heart; your heart light orb expands around you, filling your aura, your mind, body, and spirit, filling out your etheric wings and angelic halo.

You shine as the angelic being you authentically are, and shift in a moment into this creator state, this angelic state where you choose to change, to embody the higher vibrational state and quality, and to align with what you are manifesting as a creator being for your benefit, yes, and for the benefit of all.

Your family, friends, and the collective are all served by your embodying this higher vibrational truth, by your choosing to live in the new earth, in this higher vibrational paradigm of experience.

With your heart open, light turned on and shining bright, you respond to every situation as the angelic creator being, as your natural divine human state. You choose to change altered states of negative emotion, fear, and anxiety as they arise, and to be aware that these are not you or your authentic truth.

By choosing to recognize them for that which they are—limited constructs of illusion—you step back and elevate into a beautiful and empowered state, your creator state.

Here you are linked through your open heart, throat, third eye, crown, soul star direct to Source. Allow yourself to connect to your power in the light, in this new paradigm, and claim your ability to live inspired and awake in every moment, to live as the divine being you authentically are.

As you experience a series of progressive moments in this state, much will open for you. You are in alignment with receiving your gifts of creator source, your talents as an angelic human, your skills, abilities, and power in the light.

You will make a difference in your ability to serve, cocreate, and thrive by choosing to change, shift, and return to this state of embodiment.

Also in this state, with your heart open, shining your full light, we invite you to connect with the crystalline grid of the awakened earth, to download the codes of awakening, the activations, and divine frequency available to you now.

Feel increased light streaming into your heart, your crown, your third eye, your throat, elevating you further. Light streams into every cell, activating your DNA, restoring the higher vibrational divine qualities of your being and the divine template for your being divine human.

Receive and download these codes of awakening.

And now, through your heart and hands, let yourself feel your codes of awakening flowing forth, contributing to the human heart grid and the collective consciousness to share your peace in the collective awakening, unfoldment, and return to divine humanity.

Receive, light up, and flow forth.

You are in a mastery state, and are now able to return to, change back into, and restore this mastery state at any time. This is why you are here, and why we are connecting together now.

We are honored to welcome you to the table into a higher dimensional experience of light; you, at first, consciously choose to return here to your elevated state, which is your natural state.

You change lower emotional responses by observing, embodying, and shifting into your angelic human form until this state of being becomes natural for you to embody in every moment. This is your opportunity as the gateway doors open the embodiment of your divine truth, higher self, and authentic state.

We love you and are here to assist and serve you. Ask for help and claim your empowerment, your higher vibrational divine state. We honor and bless you.

And as we step back our frequency, we invite your higher self to step forward even more.

Now continue to embody your highest light as you, divine being, angelic being, step forward awakened, empowered, reunited with your authentic light, your natural state of being in the new day, the new earth, this new level of light.

Know that you are a way-shower in this.

Your presence and embodiment are paving the way for more of humanity to make this journey. Continue to shine with your heart open, your mind clear, and your angelic energy intact.

Shine, light up, glow, and freely flow your love forth, choosing to change out of lower states as needed and retain this higher level, your divine light.

We love you; we honor and bless you.

And so, it is . . .

9 OPENING THE GATEWAY OF LIGHT

Greetings from the Council of Light …

Indeed, we are present with you in this very moment now in which you are listening.

We greet you outside of time and space to meet you in the ever-present now, the point of your power, the entrance into the infinite, the point and place in which you are now able to enter inward to experience a profound unfoldment, a profound entrance into a new vibrational level of light.

We invite you, if you are willing, to shift into a new higher timeline of possibility so that you may experience the profound embodiment of your highest level of divine light and authenticity. We invite you to embody your higher self and to live as the fully awakened light being in physical form you came here to Earth to be.

And now, as synthetic timelines and layers of illusion have melted away, the gateway for your becoming, for your returning to the full embodiment of your highest potential is opening.

We are honored for this opportunity to prepare you for this shift now, soothing your emotional being, awakening your aura and light, reassuring your mind that although there is much unknown before you, it is in the unknown that the known reappears.

The level of knowingness that awaits you is profound as you transcend the dualistic battle of light and dark, as you ascend beyond the soul experience of duality into the divine neutrality, and as you experience true harmony and possibility and radiant future.

This is an opportunity for you to embody your full divine awareness, seeing the bigger picture, knowing the full truth, feeling your infinite light and potential, seeing beyond the veil of illusion, and experiencing and embodying your radiant joy and bliss and serenity and harmony and wisdom and clarity as a light being fully embodied in physical form.

A part of this preparation is cleansing the layers of pain and frustration and dense emotion and mental constructs and fear tied to the illusion, tied to the duality, tied to the programmed response to challenges as a physical being.

These are all tied to illusion, for the underlying truth and reality of the situation is your direct link to the Infinite, to Source, to the greater divine presence of God, to the underlying oneness and unity that you—through the full embodiment of your highest self, of your light being self—are able to recognize.

Although there is underlying unity, in the realm in which you live, there is separation. This is your experience.

And so, returning to the full knowing of this unity requires the full awakening of your individuality, which means peeling back the programming of a society pointing you in the opposite direction. It means peeling back the programming of illusion, of smallness, of fear and insecurity and lower levels of emotion.

Your guardian angels and your light team step forward to support you in this, in peeling the layers back to reveal the innate brilliance, the inner light.

As layers peel away, feel yourself letting go as if a limiting part—a negative part, a fear-based part—of yourself is leaving, allowing the inner light to more brightly shine through, allowing the inner authenticity and truth to reemerge, allowing the diamond light, the golden light, the divine light of love and wisdom and purity and brilliance that always shines within you to be rekindled and to ignite at a new level.

The light within you—now unhampered by the layers of illusion suppressing its brilliance—is able to radiantly shine.

And outward from your heart, let this aura of love, this flame of brilliance, this light of the infinite expand around you.

Let yourself expand with it as you embody all that you are, as you embody the unique qualities of your soul and higher self, as you embody the awakened divine blueprint of your infinite possibility.

Your spiritual gifts and psychic abilities and divine cosmic awareness click into place through this simple perspective of shining within.

Remain undamped by layers of illusion around, so that the light can expand, the divine presence flow forth, and the divine blueprint become reinstated in this moment now.

A waterfall of light begins to stream in around you—each droplet, a different color—every color of the visible and non-visible spectrum. This cosmic rainbow light is flowing all around you in a steady and consistent stream, rushing around you, releasing the residue of density and duality, lifting you further.

And now, imagine a disc of light lowering down around you, around your being, creating a pillar around you. The divine light of perfection in this disc lowers down all the way along your spine, down through your hips and legs, down through your knees and calves, down through your ankles and the bones in your feet and toes, down about 12 inches below your feet where it clicks into place.

As this disc of golden rainbow ultraviolet light clicks into place, notice the pattern upon it, the flower of life, the template for creation, a symbol of the divine phase of creation you are about to enter.

And upward from this disc of light, from the flower of light, a brilliant pillar of divine presence, of golden diamond platinum rainbow light, expands around you, opening the gateway to the higher realms.

It opens the gateway to the Galactic center through which the codes of awakening, the activations to your DNA, the technological upgrades to your physical body, the harmonization of your mind, a mental recalibration, and the upliftment of your spirit all flow forth.

As this gateway is opened in your present point in time, feel the rush of energy from the Galactic center. Feel the downloads through waves of light from the Divine. Feel the light and presence of the Infinite flowing into your every cell, refreshing you on every level and elevating you in this present moment now.

And as this gateway fully opens, more love flows into your each and every cell.

The golden light all around you also flows within, so that your every cell embodies your highest divine qualities; your every organ and every structure of your physical body is recalibrated with this infinite divine light.

The mental constructs, the beliefs or patterns of thought tying you to aging—tying you to these older paradigms of limitation—are resolved and healed. The belief of well-being and vitality and harmony and immortality are reinstated, for these are the qualities of your soul and you are becoming the full brilliance of your soul embodied.

Let the light that glows within your heart expand upward and downward simultaneously. The golden light is like a tube along your entire being, connecting you to the brilliance of the earth core below and the brilliance of the Galactic center above.

These two streams of light—from the crystalline core of Gaia below, from the crystalline center of the galaxy above—now meet within. They meet within your diamond heart light.

Your crystalline heart light opens the doors to a new paradigm of possibility for your radiant wellbeing, your vibrant potential, to sync with the highest level of your divine light and in awareness of your direct link with Source.

Bask in this love as the direct downloads through this gateway flow into your present point in time, as they flow into the earth, into your home, and into your physical proximity.

As you embody this divine signature of your authenticity and your highest truth, all whom you encounter are blessed through your presence, for you carry this field of love. And this field of love you carry activates the unique codes and frequencies of your soul.

Activating yourself to your highest potential is stepping forward as the One, the Way, the full embodiment of the individual you are who, as an individual, is a core piece of the One.

You are a unique particle of creation, a divine spark, an essential piece of the whole.

And as the full embodiment of your divine authenticity,

you are able to return to the whole, to the awareness, to the experience of yourself as infinite, as one with Source and one with All, free from the judgments of separation, free from the over-analysis or fear to simply bask in the light, in the unity and divine perfection.

The gateway is open and you have now received a glimpse of embodying your highest divine blueprint, the ninth-dimensional pattern of perfection for you as an individual in the physical.

Before we step away, let us experience now together another surge of light from the Infinite and from the Divine streaming through this gateway into your present point in time. Ripples of light expand around, shining the blessings of the Divine and the pattern of perfection, the sacred geometric progression of the highest manifestation of your light.

Every area of your life expands around you from this point in time, so that the path before you is paved with love and wisdom and harmony, so that your next steps are clearly revealed.

Tune into the concentrated supply of light in your heart and become aware of this heart light now shining with more brilliance than you have ever experienced. Imagine that this light of the divine and love is expanding in every direction.

It flows above you, activating your higher chakras and opening these centers. It flows below you, sealing your lower chakras, so that you are not pulled into a lower vibrational experience.

And as the light of your heart extends above and below, it also equally expands around wide, bringing love and divine presence and infinite brilliance into all areas of your life, into all your encounters, all your relationships, all your opportunities.

The path before you is truly paved. And as this light continues to flow out beyond you, let yourself honor and feel and experience how vast the potential for you as an individual really is.

The limitations you have felt and the fears you have felt and the doubt you have experienced are simply remnants of the illusion and of the experience of polarity, but the underlying truth is this embodied state of love that we now hand-in-hand step forward into together.

We step into a new phase of unfoldment, into a new timeline, into your highest embodiment of love, fulfillment, and co-creation, aware of your place and direct link within the Infinite.

Experience yourself as vast, as infinite, tuning into the light within you. And now, into the vast light and space and divine presence all around, expand wide, tall, deep, and far.

Now, as you return to your body, know that you are returning to a new body and in a new place and a new point in time. Step forward on your new path, on your new timeline, into your new reality in which you are in sync, in the flow, in a state of divine synchronicity and understanding.

Your intuition is on point, your guidance clearly revealed, your next step brightly illuminated. As you take that step, then the next will appear as you ascend and embody all that you are and the vast potential available to you which, yes, has been hidden from your eyes, but which is now revealed.

Step forward into the new and receive the downloads of the Divine that await, for you are now prepared for what is next in this new realm where your infinite possibility has become fully available.

The light of love within you aligns you with the possibility of your highest potential and with the highest blueprint and most benevolent outcome for you as an individual embodied and living as divine light in the physical.

We are honored to serve and support and assist. We love and will continue to guide. We will meet you again soon, but for now we are complete.

Return to your new timeline, refreshed and reinvigorated and knowing just how loved you really are and just how miraculous you really are and just how vast the opportunity is before you, as you step up into embodying your highest love and most vibrant light.

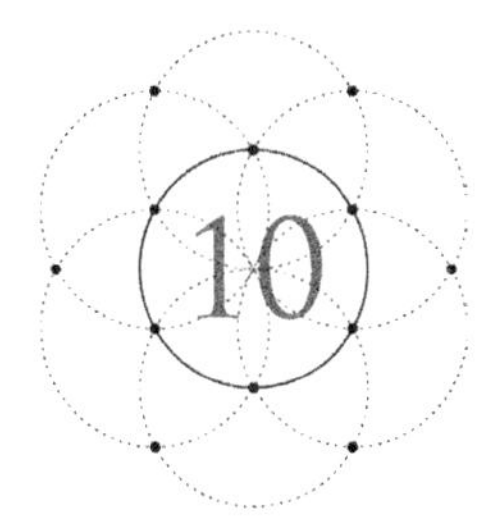

1111 GATEWAY

We are honored to connect with you now, to assist you in calling forth this gateway portal and stepping through the 1111 portal into greater sync and harmony with your full soul light.

This 1111 gateway opens the possibilities for your direct communication with the spiritual realms, allowing a greater access to the higher dimensional realms of spirit and light.

It is enabling you to call in and forth the activations that are right for you, that you may step into alignment, into sync with the higher level of your soul authenticity embodying your higher self, embodying your soul light, embodying your divine self on your highest possible ascension timeline to usher in and call forth the most benevolent outcomes with grace and ease ... in alignment with the highest interest of all.

And so, in preparation for this 1111 gateway activation, we invite you to focus inward, to breathe, relax, and let go as a greater level of divine light flows in on the 12 divine rays, elevating the vibration of your space and supporting you in letting go of the external, letting go of the lines of time, letting go and entering inward.

To do this, relax your hands, the bones in your hands, your fingers, relax your arms, relax your feet, calves and legs, relaxing to allow the light in.

As you relax your hands, they are filling up with light.

As you relax your feet, your feet are illuminated.

Relax your ankles as light in a counterclockwise motion now begins to spiral around and up from below your feet, cleansing your connection to the collective consciousness, spiraling around in this counterclockwise motion around your ankles, releasing any form of attachment, releasing any connection to the pain body, releasing all that no longer serves you.

And as you allow a new level of light in, as this vortex of divine light spirals around you, let go.

Release energy and attachment. Release to cleanse and expand your being as this golden spiral of light from the crystalline core descends, supported by your team of guides and angels.

It spirals around your ankles, your legs and knees, flowing into your knees, releasing any and all resistance into the light.

Let go, as it continues spiraling around your hips and waist, your abdomen; spiraling around your chest, your heart, your throat, your shoulders; spiraling around your head, light flowing into your mind, into your brain; spiraling around the top of your head, spiraling around your upper chakra energy centers.

This golden spiral of light spiraling around you in a counterclockwise motion now accelerates, spinning faster to cleanse as you purge and release any memories that no longer support you and the emotions and energy tied to past or future lines of time.

Let go and release all that you are not required to carry forward into the new, into the new earth.

Let go of the old, let go of the heavy, let go of the dense, let go of the pain, let go of resistance.

Breathe in the light and on this exhale, let go and release to shine brighter, tuning into your heart light. Tune into the space behind your heart to find a stillness, a calm amidst this vortex of light which continues to spin around you.

And yet, you are able to enter into your center, to your open heart where you are met with an incredible brilliant light and the complete feeling of peace and tranquility.

Tune into the space inside your heart, the vast space that opens up inside you. And from this heart-centered place, your guardian angel steps forward to guide and protect you through this entire experience.

Your inner child, in their complete purity and innocence and brilliant light, steps forward with an open heart to receive.

And now, the light from the crystalline core of the ascended earth streams upward, in through the bottom of your feet, activating and flowing up along your ascension column. As you breathe in, feel the light flow up, flowing up into your heart, into your throat, into your third eye, into your brain, activating your crown and your direct link to the Divine.

You may now imagine a figure-eight spiral of light uniting the left and right hemispheres of your brain. The light circulates and spirals through your brain, cleansing your pineal, activating your pituitary and hypothalamus, and opening this cave of Christos, this energetic function of allowing the flow of higher dimensional light, high vibrational manifestation.

Your highest ascension is now ushered forth.

And as this infinity figure-eight of light flows, uniting the hemispheres of your brain, once again, tune into your heart light which expands around you, expanding heart light around your being.

Relax and focus on that still point energy, the zero-point field where you are connected to the infinite realm of consciousness, the vast field of infinite divine God light, source field, infinite possibility.

And now, aware of this vast field of light, this vast space all around you and within you that you are a part of, four columns of light surround you.

The archangelic energy of the 1111 portal enters in and these columns of pure white light create a sacred sanctuary for this experience, aligning in the North, South, East, and West, extending all the way down to the crystalline core of Gaia, anchoring and grounding this space on the highest possible ascension timeline.

These crystalline columns of light extend upward into direct presence with source God divine, extending up and arcing in to unite as one, to create the sacred space, this sacred container for pure crystalline consciousness, for accelerated awakening, for expanded awareness, for pure divine consciousness to enter in.

As this crystalline temple—the four pillars of light—are constructed around you, feel the warmth and tranquility and peace and serenity of this divine space you have co-created by being here now, which you have called in and forth.

And in this space, in the presence of the archangels, the seraphim, we—the Council of Light and your entire team of guides, guardians, star family, ascended beings, all of the highest light and integrity acting in the highest interest of all—assist you now in receiving through your open heart, through the innocence and purity of your inner child, the light, the activation, the download and divine transmission of crystalline consciousness, the codes of your highest awakening, your true divine nature resurrected and revealed.

Receive this light transmission, this blessing through your

open heart, lifting, expanding, the light flowing into every cell, the light flowing into the space between your cells, into your DNA, activating your gifts, your highest possibilities, aligning you with your highest divine ascension timeline and the opportunities in alignment with your highest joy and fulfillment, radiant service and incredible brilliant love.

At this time, you may become aware of your entire body glowing with the crystalline light.

The chakras in your hands and feet are activated as you receive and send forth the blessings of this awakened consciousness, receiving and flowing forth for the well-being and benefit of all.

You may become aware of your etheric wings and the expansive nature of your light as before you now, the gateway, the door of this 1111 portal appears, appearing before you as the 11, the initiation, the doorway.

You are invited to step up, step forward, step into this new level of embodying your highest light in every moment, rippling out through your entire experience.

Become aware of this 1111 gateway, the door held up by the seraphim, the archangels. Feel the warmth and bliss radiating in this space.

And with your heart open, your inner child aspect intact, your innocence and willingness and joy and excitement reinvigorated and restored, step forward, stepping through this gateway into the new, into the light, into resonance and harmony with the divine tone of Source God creation.

Listen for this tone with your inner ears.

Listen to receive this recalibration, harmonizing your entire life with the divine blueprint of your awakened divine being.

Become aware of the color of light all around you, the golden rainbow diamond platinum light nurturing you on every level and preparing you to receive the next level of your soul embodiment. Receiving this download through your open heart now, re-center your awareness at the still point of your heart behind your heart center.

Become aware now of your highest divine self who has been here with you all along, but in this new level of frequency and awareness, you are able to merge with, to directly connect with, to receive their guidance, blessing, and incredible love.

If it serves you now, they may share their name or a tone to help you harmonize. You may see their presence, know or feel the profound synchronicity of this connection right here and now, for your rising up and embodying this high level of light cannot be undone.

In other words, the benefits and positive implications are being called forth in the form of new opportunities, new alignments and synchronicities, peace and understanding empowered through this, your divine connection.

In this space, in this high vibrational state, you are unaffected by lower dimensional forms who quite simply cannot elevate to this level of vibrational frequency.

And so, if there are times, moving forward, where your vibration drops down and you feel affected by trickster energy or negativity, remember the simple process of invoking light around you, visualizing the counterclockwise spiral of golden light to cleanse your energy, to elevate your vibrational form.

Then, through your open heart, your crystalline ascension column of light, lift up. And with your heart open, shine to shift inward and upward into this vibrational alignment with your higher dimensional divinity, understanding that as a multidimensional being, you have a divine aspect.

This pathway and doorway through this 1111 gateway has been opened and you have stepped through. And on the other side, we celebrate all that you are, all that you have been, all the challenging times you've been through across timelines.

And now, centered in your open heart, linked with the divine presence, aware of the infinite possibility and knowing that all is well, we welcome you home into this divine presence that you are.

We love you, we bless you, we honor you as you now carry this vibrational frequency back into your physical body, bringing a new level of light into every cell, bringing a new level of vitality into every cell, bringing a new level of serenity and understanding and tranquility into your mind, bringing awareness into the present.

As you return your focus to your heart center, become aware of the link between heart, throat, third eye, crown—this crystalline column opening.

Any blockages in the throat or third eye release to allow the divine energetic flow from the crystalline core of Gaia below your feet, up along your ascension column into the direct presence with Divine Source above.

The flow is spiraling around you like a waterfall of light, this beautiful toroidal energy field which accelerates, amplifies, and expands. It fills your aura, your room, your home, your country, and the entire earth with divine light and presence.

The blessings of this opening will continue to be revealed as you remain present. And with your heart open, your energy flowing in its divine form, you choose to be aware, to be present, to release the small voice of ego or fear, knowing you are so much more.

Tune into your higher, multidimensional, divine state of being. View through this lens, knowing that all is well and knowing that you are now being supported in stepping into a higher level of your divine light work and service.

Your intuition and inspiration, your guardian angel, your

higher self, the pure divine light and presence of your soul will guide you.

Awareness, presence, open heart … this is how you tune in.

We love you, we honor you, we bless you. All is well.

Take a moment to return awareness to your physical body, knowing that you have now returned to your highest possible timeline which with your open heart and your energy flowing in divine accordance can unfold in the highest interest of all, with grace, ease, harmony and beauty.

And so, it is …

Thank you, thank you, thank you…

Thank you.

11 STEPPING THROUGH THE GATEWAY

We are now beginning to elevate the quality of light around you, purifying the energy of your space and working with you as an individual to restore you in this present moment, bringing you into alignment and into sync with the highest possible vibration of your unique soul tone.

Like a divine tuning fork, you are being realigned and recalibrated to your highest level of divine authenticity, so that you are able to reset into a higher dimension of light and a higher vibrational experience.

And so, as light bands flow in on every ray, let yourself relax, knowing that you are safe and supported, you are loved and uplifted, you are in the presence of your entire team who nurture, protect, love, and uplift you now.

We are supporting you in entering inward, letting go of the focus on the external, letting go of focus on your surroundings, on your timeline, on your history, on your future.

Let go of thought and enter inward, focusing your attention on your heart.

And where your attention goes, your energy flows and

your heart begins to open.

Enter inward. Relax and go within, tuning into light glowing at your center, the center of your being, your heart chakra filling with golden diamond rainbow light, purifying and uplifting you from the inside out, so that this light now extends around you in a beautiful orb.

Focus on the light around you, the light around your heart center, around your physical being, the light filling your aura, the light filling your room. And in this light, let yourself vibrationally lift.

Relax your body as another influx of light meets you in this present point in time, light flowing in from above, in from below, in from all around, uplifting you.

Lift up in the light. Lift up in vibration. Lift up in awareness from within this inner focused state of being. Lift up, way up into the light at the center of the galaxy.

Imagine you are in this place. The light of the great central sun brightly shines all around you, revealing areas of stuck or stagnant energy, revealing limiting beliefs in this brilliant golden light, revealing that which no longer serves you.

And with your willingness now, you are able to let it go.

Release into the light.

Release limitation, release uncertainty, release attachment, release that which has been to make way for a higher vibrational experience that is entirely new.

Become aware of the vast space of the light around you, the vastness of the light all around your being. You are at the center of this light, allowing you to receive healing, to receive a recalibration, allowing you to reset.

Imagine that the light is entering into your every cell. Imagine it pouring in through your crown chakra at the top of your head, in through your hands, in through your feet, in through your spinal column, into every cell. Notice where you end and the divine light around you begins.

And now, let any separation, any barrier be dissolved, so that you are able to become aware of your oneness with this divine light, of yourself as divine light, shining as the great central sun, shining as the brightest source of light.

And as you simply shine this starlight, this sunlight forth, let it raise your vibration, cleanse your being on every level, and fully restore your authentic vibrational energetic signature.

A part of this is elevating your vibration, integrating this light into every cell; and a part of this is letting go of whatever scattered, disorganized, or fragmented functions of the lower vibration you are still carrying.

There is simultaneously a feeling of leaving, of letting go, of releasing and receiving, integrating, absorbing.

And now from your heart, the center of your being, tune into the highest vibration of light, the purest divine presence that you carry within.

Your heart center is cleansed. Your inner light, your full vibrance, is restored. Shining forth as the central sunshine, your light shines forth. Your love shines forth the energy of blessing, of gratitude, of compassion, of peace, of harmony.

Your heart is flowing light forth, connecting to the human heart grid, the hearts of all awakened humanity uniting as one now, elevating the vibration further, elevating the vibration of humanity, of earth through this infusion of love.

And now, as you are connected to the human heart grid, receive the download of your highest level of authenticity. Receive the download of your divine blueprint, the codes of awakening and the frequencies of the divine, of the light.

Receive this light into your heart, integrated into your being, assimilated into your cells.

And now, flow it forth.

Not holding on or grasping, but allowing your awakened light to flow through you. You are a channel, a conduit of your highest light and potential, so that you receive it. It elevates your vibration and you share it forth, elevating the vibration of humanity and the consciousness of all.

Receive the unique codes of awakening, the light imprints, the divine blueprint of your highest authenticity. Receive this divine download streaming in like a waterfall of light around you.

Receive it. And now, through your heart and through your hands, send this forth to the human heart grid. This receiving and giving, this magic of service elevates your vibration even more, so that you are now able to connect to the crystalline grid, the higher dimensional grid of Gaia, Mother Earth.

Connect with the crystalline grid now and receive the codes of awakening, the ascension updates, the downloads available to you now.

Receive them into your heart, in through your hands, in through your feet, into your being.

Receive the blessing, the love, the recalibration, the divine knowledge and wisdom and information.

Receive the light.

And your team of guides and angels, your higher selves, assist you in assimilating and integrating this light into your body, into your cellular memory, into your DNA, activating you now as the divine human you authentically are, activating your golden Christed light, your diamond light, your rainbow light body to the highest degree that is possible for you now.

Shine as the divine embodiment of light, of spirit in the physical.

And now, shine forth these codes of awakening, this love and presence, sharing what you have received with the human heart grid, with the earth, with all of humanity.

This selfless service through love opens the gateway of light around you, which you may become aware of as a vast pillar of golden or rainbow light. An orb of light lowers down along your being, down all the way to the crystalline core of Gaia.

This orb of light carrying the divine geometric form of Metatron's Cube, the sacred geometry, lowers down and clicks into place at the center of the globe, directly below your feet.

Feel this disc, this orb, this Metatronic cube click into place.

And as it does, the gateway of light opens. It is the doorway into the next level of your experience, the next level of your divine service, your inspired living, your passionate living, your vibrant well-being.

The threshold into this new dimension of your experience is open. Your team of guides and angels all step forward, taking you by the hands, placing their hands on your back and shoulders, so that you know how loved and supported you really are—in letting go of the old, in letting go of what has been, in letting go of limitations.

And now—hand-in-hand with your team supported by the divine, stepping through the gateway of light—imagine yourself stepping forward, stepping through the waterfall of light, into alignment with the highest dimension of your authentic soul experience, into sync with the new levels of light and opportunity available to you.

You are stepping into the new paradigm, a new dimension.

In this space now, become aware of a feeling of lightness, a feeling of renewal.

Feel loved, refreshed, uplifted, and supported as we, the Council of Light, now surround you, flowing forth from our hearts to yours the divine qualities of love and illumination, the codes of mastery and divine frequencies of love that will most support you in embodying your highest light and potential in this new timeline, this new dimension you've stepped into.

Be willing to turn a page.

Be willing to reset.

Be willing to step fully into this new beginning where you are aware of your infinite potential, where you are in tune and in alignment with your light and power, where you clearly know your purpose, where you serve with love and authenticity and you stand in your full power and light.

Here, you are empowered to take the reins and claim your power as a divine sovereign being in physical form, shining with light and divine presence and creating a magnificent ripple of love out beyond you.

From this present point in time, you—connected to the crystalline grid, connected to the human heart grid—receive the divine downloads of inspiration and awakening.

You receive the download of your highest divine blueprint.

Embody your divine self now. And through this, divine blessing flows forth towards the earth, elevating the vibration of Gaia. It flows forth towards humanity, elevating the vibration of the collective consciousness.

And you—shining with your divine authenticity, your heart open, your ears open, your eyes open, your crown open—align fully with the guidance of your higher divine self, carrying this divinity within and flowing forth this golden diamond rainbow light into all areas of the new life you are about to step into, the new life you are about to create, the new paradigm, the new earth, your new reality with greater love, greater harmony, greater balance, increased vitality and increased love.

You have stepped into this new empowered state of being.

You have stepped through the gateway of light and reset into a higher level of authenticity, into a higher level of your divine expression.

Become aware of your heart center glowing with light.

Become aware of your aura and light body shining brilliantly. Become aware of your physical body glowing from the inside out. Know that your authentic vibration, your divine soul tone, your radiance, your light, your truth has been restored.

The full implications of this activation may take months or even years to fully unfold; you may not notice a shift right away. And we encourage you to simply embody the fullness and truth of that which you authentically are.

You are a unique thread in the tapestry of consciousness.

Your unique skills and abilities, and light are essential components. It's required for the full activation of the human heart grid and the entrance, the arrival of all humanity into this new paradigm.

You're living in sync with it by staying in alignment with love, by staying in alignment with your authenticity, by keeping your heart open and your light turned on. This paves the pathway for all.

Your arrival is right on time. Your being here now is no mistake. We honor the divine being you authentically are and remind you that you are able to embody more of this divinity in the physical now.

This is the threshold you have crossed.

This is the gateway you have passed through.

This is the paradigm you have entered.

And so, allow yourself to be this new divine being. Allow yourself to let go of the limitations of the past and to recognize and validate the new experience that is possible for you now. The love in your heart and light in your field and intention in your mind open you to the infinite possibility.

What is it you want to call forth in this new experience? Greater abundance? Harmony? Health? Vitality? Love?

Focus now on a single intention, a possibility from the vast field of infinite possibility that you are calling forth.

Focus upon this in your mind. And now, let this intention drop down into your heart and let yourself feel what it would be like to have this. Feel the gratitude for this that already is. Feel gratitude for your intention manifest.

And with this, your intention is beginning to be created into being.

The vibrational seed has been planted and now, you as a divine being—knowing you are able to create this, believing it already is and already exists, feeling the gratitude, the joy, the celebration of your intention manifest into being and as a divine being in physical form—now what action step can you take?

What massive action can you take in alignment with this manifestation, with this intention?

Bring your thought, word, action, and feeling into vibrational alignment with your intention. Fueled by the energy of this new paradigm and new level of light through balanced masculine and feminine action, receiving your intention is woven into being.

Whatever the specific intention, the gratitude you feel, the positive emotion you feel—the positive vibrational wavelength that you send forth in this moment and in every moment—is powerful light work.

It is a part of your service to humanity. It is a part of your service in simply maintaining a state of love, holding the field of love and light, remembering your divine sovereign nature that you are able to choose.

Choose to shift. Choose to return to love.

Choose to release the old. Choose to disengage with the drama. Choose to embody your highest divine light and then witness and experience the blessings, the magic, the possibility that is in store.

Tune into the light in your heart, the light filling your entire spinal column in a column, a pillar, a tube of light. Become aware of your divine life force energy, the crystalline life force energy spiraling all around you, flowing in alignment with divine perfection, in alignment with your highest divine blueprint.

And this divine flow of life force ushers forth healing. This flow of divine life force empowers your further awakening, the further activation of your gifts and abilities and strengths as a unique divine being—an authentic, empowered light being in physical form.

Shine your light forth.

Serve with love.

Give freely.

This service, this light-free high vibration elevates you even more.

And still hand in hand, you with your team of guides and angels and ascended masters—as a soul family, as equals—anchor the new paradigm of high vibrational dimensional light into this moment, into the present point in time, into the crystalline grid, into the human heart grid, into your spirit, your emotional being, your aura, your physical body, your every cell buzzing and shining with coherent love and divine light.

This coherence rewrites the reality around you. Your returning to love rewrites what is in store.

You are truly reset into a new beginning. So, do not dwell on what has been. Rather, now think and be and act and vibrate and resonate and be in alignment with your highest light, with your core intentions, with that which you seek.

This being in alignment creates and you create. You—as a thread in the tapestry, as a player in the symphony, as an essential piece of the puzzle—raise the vibration of your proximity.

And together, we raise the collective consciousness. We raise the vibration of earth and all.

You are immensely loved and supported. You are celebrated. You are honored. You are blessed.

We love you and we encourage you to shine, to vibrate your unique soul tone in its magnificence and beauty and clarity, free from distortion, free from limitation, in perfect sync with the infinite divine light that you are a part of and that you are toning in perfect coherence with now.

We leave you now with a final surge of light, of love, and our blessing.

Shine forth the full love that you are. And return to your physical body, to a new body in a new point in time, to a new opportunity with the full awareness of the infinite possibility before you and the power and opportunity you have to call your specific intention forth.

Stand in the full light of your divinity.

Stand empowered as the light being in physical form you are.

Shine forth your light. And through service and love and presence and vibrating with your unique tone, the path will continue to appear. You will continue to progress.

This is not the end.

This is a reset and a new beginning, so that you, now more than ever, can more vibrantly, more authentically, more joyfully, more lovingly shine.

We now leave you with our blessing, with a stream of light from each of the 12 rays, bringing you into harmony, into perfect coherence, into love.

You are able to stay in this present, centered high vibrational state, illuminated, joyful and loving. And if you fall out of it, if you trip, simply shift. Return to your heart, ignite your light, embodying the fullness of the light being you are. For now we are complete.

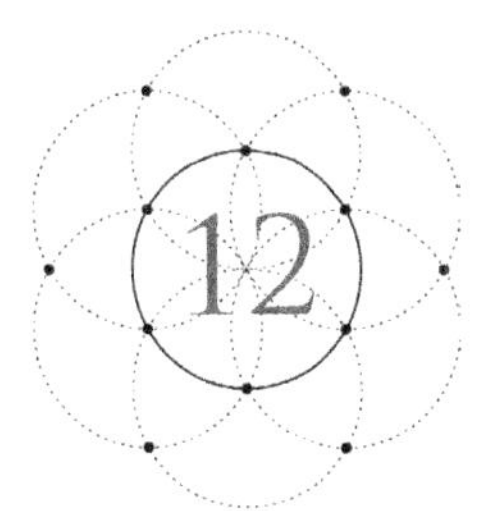

CARRYING THE 1111 ENERGY

At this time, let yourself focus within as light and divine presence flow all around.

Breathe, relax, and begin to tune into the presence of divine love by shifting your awareness into the center of your being, into your heart center, tuning into light.

As you breathe and relax, this light expands outward from your heart. Golden light flows into your entire body—golden light flowing out to fill your aura, your energy body, and the room you are in.

Relax, breathe, and expand, being fully present in this moment, tuned in to the incredible love and light and healing energy that is all around.

Relax your body; relax your mind.

Let go of the external; let go of time; let go of what you have done; let go of what you have to do.

Let go, relax, and enter inward as four pillars of divine light now surround you. These pillars reach down all the way to the core of Gaia where they arc into one still center point.

And these divine pillars of light reach up to the heavens, again arcing in towards one another to reach a single point, creating around you this sacred space and opening. This cocoon of light now fills with the energy of tranquility, harmony, peace, and love, elevating the vibration of your space and elevating your vibration by being here now.

As you breathe in, breathe light into every cell of your body. And as you exhale, let go and lift in the light that is all around you.

Lift on the wings of angels who are supporting you now in raising your vibration, in calling forth well-being and blessings through your presence, through simply being in the midst of this incredible frequency that is all around you.

In this sacred space—surrounded by the pillars of light—become aware of the archangelic energy, aware of the presence of your team of guides, angels, and ascended masters stepping forward to assist you now in stepping through.

Step once again through the 1111 portal that appears before you, a doorway of brilliant light, golden light spiraling around you, cleansing the energy, cleansing you in this present point in time.

This light is readying you and preparing you to step up and step forward and step into alignment with your true divine nature and birthright, your ability to receive direct divine guidance, your ability to connect and commune with the divine, to hear and see the angels, to know your higher selves and to call forth healing, well-being, abundance, love.

The unique ascension downloads meant for you to carry in this life await you now.

The keys meant for you to embody and shine forth are waiting for you in every moment. They are waiting for you to simply tune in, to shift your perspective from the physical to the infinite.

This is the gift the 1111 doorway offers you now, inviting you to step through it into the new, your personal new beginning, into a new level of your authenticity, where you stand in your power.

Align with your gifts. Shine your light forth.

Make a difference as a way-shower here in the physical. Make a difference through vibrantly living your life well.

Serving and loving others is not missing out at all. It aligns you with the best of what is in store, for it brings you into sync with your true divine blueprint of infinite possibility.

Having stepped through this doorway, through this 1111 gateway portal, tune into the space all around your body and the light all around you, glistening and sparkling and spiraling with divine perfection.

Feel your oneness with this light and let your awareness expand even more.

Tune into the vastness of creation, the vastness of the infinite, the vast space and light and divine presence all around you. Expand into it.

And now, once again, focus your awareness at the center of your being, the center of your heart.

All of this power of the Infinite, of the Divine, of the vast field that makes up All That Is—the incredible light and love and power all around you—compresses down. It condenses in for you to access in every moment inside of your radiant, glowing, awakened heart.

Let your heart burst open to a new degree. Let the light travel upward from your heart into your throat which opens your mind's eye, which opens your crown, which opens and continues up.

Lift up.

Embody the soul light that you are.

Live as the awakened divine being you are, here to live vibrantly well, to thrive, to love, to serve others, to make a difference, to thoroughly enjoy.

The divine light of the 1111 portal represents your direct connection with the divine; it represents your ability to download all that you need—knowledge, wisdom, truth, healing, light, frequency, love, and guidance.

All of this and more are offered to you freely, for you to receive willingly.

The divine blessings of the infinite realm of possibility flow into your heart, into your ascension column along the spine, into your aura, light body, into your space.

Let your body, mind, spirit, space be blessed in the way that will most serve with the opportunities and possibilities and connections and joyous occurrences that most serve according to your divine blueprint.

Let these blessings align now. Know that they have, so in this moment, you are in alignment.

Let go of the doubt and worry.

Let go of fear of failure. Let go of fear and frustration. Let go and embrace your destiny to live and to co-create with the infinite field of All That Is, staying focused on your intentions and open for the blessings and surprises and infinite possibility for things to unfold in a way that's even better than you could expect.

Intend ... call forth what you want, but leave an opening for something that's even better, for things to unfold even more magically, more radiantly, more beautifully than you could have imagined.

Know that this is what is possible when you trust, when you sync, when you align with the divine nature of time.

Open your heart, letting your ascension column fill with light, giving you an expanded awareness centered in love. Embodying the light in this way creates powerful waves out beyond you.

You have a role in what transpires in your future. Choose the most benevolent outcome by continuing to return to divine presence, shining your light and holding the field of love.

And through your open heart, receive now from the Divine and from the Infinite, the blessings of love and light that will most serve.

Receive the energy, the color, the qualities that you most need. Download these now into your being, direct from Source, Divine, God, All That Is.

Receive direct from the Divine, direct from Source, direct from the crystalline grid, direct from the central sun. Let the light fill you.

Know that each time you see 1111 or any number sequence that catches your eye, this is a signal to return to this present moment awareness, to open your heart, to let your energy flow along your ascension column, to let light fill your being.

In these moments, the codes of awakening, the guidance, the wisdom and opportunities are within reach. Through your open heart and clear mind, you are able to receive and tune in.

We are with you in every moment, guiding you, encouraging you, supporting you.

Keep choosing love as you continue further on your path, knowing that all is well, that you are vibrant in your full authenticity and light. This is what you can call forth and embody in the present, in this moment and in every moment now.

Return to love, shining your light and receiving all that the ascension process has to show you, all that the divine has to give and reveal to you, all the many blessings of infinite possibility that are yet in store.

Listen, be present, trust, receive, and act on the guidance and inspiration that appears. And continue, for you are at a new beginning, a new beginning.

You now are on the path of stepping into your most vibrant light. Call it forth, let it shine, and know how loved you really are.

Thank you, thank you, thank you…

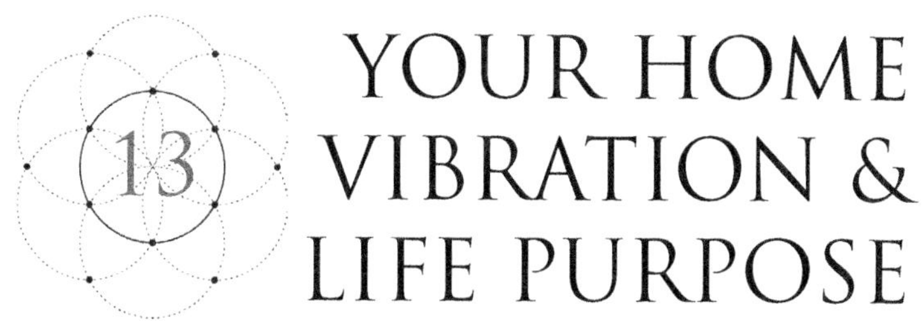

13 YOUR HOME VIBRATION & LIFE PURPOSE

Let yourself breathe, relax, and begin to focus your awareness within. Know that you are, indeed, enveloped in light, surrounded in love, uplifted in divine frequency and presence, and assisted in entering within.

Let your mind be still.

Release any thoughts that come into your awareness over to your angels and let yourself focus within. As you simply breathe, relax, and let go, tune into the stillness.

Tune into the quiet and the calm found within. Enter inward, breathe, relax and let go.

Take a deep breath in and pause. And then exhale completely and pause. Breathe in deeply ... pause ... and exhale fully and pause.

As you focus on your breathing in this way, feel your energy and your awareness returning to you at this present point in time. All the light, all the wisdom and frequency that is available to you in any moment is available to you now.

Focus within, open your heart and now imagine, once

again, a brilliant orb of light begins to lower down, containing the full essence of your higher self and your diamond light body.

Your higher self, embodying the fullness and truth of your authentic vibration, enters into this present point in time from above. Your higher self is standing behind you now, and is placing hands upon your shoulders.

Focusing internally, focusing within, you are able to effortlessly merge with the light of your higher self, with your diamond light body now.

Breathe and allow yourself to tune into the truth in frequency, the truth of the light, the truth of the authentic vibrational frequency, which is your home frequency and your authentic vibration. Return home by entering in, opening your heart and feeling the reemergence of your light, of your high vibrational essence, your authentic spiritual, light-filled vibrational truth.

Continue to breathe and relax in this very moment, as more and more of your authentic vibration enters into this space here and now.

Feel and experience the light that you are, the diamond light body, the crystalline energy, which is your authentic nature, which unites you directly with God, Divine Source, and All That Is, which intricately connects you with every aspect of creation.

You are not separate from anyone or anything. You are one.

And when you are present in your authentic vibration, you are able to recognize this underlying oneness in compassion and in love.

Allow yourself to simply continue to breathe. Relax, feel, and experience your authentic vibration and truth.

And now from above, notice a giant sun of divine energy shining down upon you—pure divine essence, pure spiritual energy and light power shining down upon you—shining down upon you as you are present in your diamond light body, in crystalline form.

And just as light shining into a crystal is reflected back, feel yourself receiving and reflecting back the pure light of the Divine, so your inner light burns and shines brightly from within and divine light pours down upon you from above.

From within, you are shining. And from without, you are reflecting.

Experience the divine light from the sun of divine energy, shining down upon you, pouring into your being from your crown chakra above the top of your head. Receive the divine light frequency, the codes of enlightenment, the crystalline attunement, and divine vibrational alignment.

And feel yourself reflect the energy of the Divine, of love, of peace, of power, of truth, of integrity, of well-being, of vitality and more.

Receive divine light and reflect divine light outward.

Breathe and experience this beautiful transfer of divine energy that you are a part of.

When you receive the divine light energy, when you are in your diamond light body form, as you are now, the divine frequency in its pure, beautiful state is amplified further, is broadcast outward, is anchored to this here and now, and ripples out far beyond you in this present moment, across the lines of time, across all of reality, across existence and nonexistence, space and void.

As you simply breathe, receive and reflect the light that you are and that shines down upon you from the golden orb of light above, the divine sun, pouring enlightenment, knowledge, and an encoded realignment of your authentic frequency upon you.

Feel your energy elevating as you receive and send light out. Feel your worries melting away, as you are fully present in this now.

And now, from above, the high vibrational ascended being who can most serve you now—in not only embodying your authentic vibration and meditation but in living the truth of your vibration in your life, in accomplishing your purpose, in living your authentic truth as a spiritual being in physical form—this high vibrational ascended guide steps forward now, steps into this time and space to serve you.

Feel their presence as they enter in.

Become aware of who this guide is, here to serve you, to stand by your side, to assist you energetically.

This guide offers you now a symbol of your fully awakened self, a symbol representing the full embodiment of your authentic vibration and spiritual being within the physical, a symbol representing how this may manifest a vibrational, metaphorical symbol of your authentic truth.

Become aware of this symbol shining before you in the light of the divine sun, reflecting the light.

The symbol is becoming brighter, glowing with an increased energy and frequency, as it embodies more divine light, more of your authentic truth and vibration, which in its very nature is high vibrational, for you are one with the Divine, with God, with your ascended guide, with your angels, with All That Is.

Your guide now plants a seed of thought—an idea, a vision, a knowing of your next steps on your path of authentic truth.

In other words, your life purpose as a spiritual being in physical form is, of course, in alignment with your authentic vibration, which is in alignment with what brings you joy and fulfillment, which is rewarding for you and offers value and service towards the collective and the greater good.

Your ascended guide helps you see a glimpse of the big picture. Even if it is tuning in to the elevated vibration, you are able to reach a glimpse of the full embodiment of your light.

And what is your next step in living in integrity with your authentic vibration and truth?

What action can you take to anchor this vibrational frequency to your physical life, to live in alignment with your authentic truth?

... Continuing on your path of awakening. Embodying more fully your spiritual light in every moment. Accomplishing the unique facets of your life purpose as a spiritual being in physical form.

They will appear consistently before you, one step at a time, and you will see your next step here and now.

Your authentic vibration can be associated with a quality of the Divine—a quality of the Divine that your higher self in spirit embodies fully and which will serve you as you embody more of this quality in your physical life.

Let your ascended guide help you tune into this quality now.

What quality most closely represents the full embodiment of your higher self and your authentic vibration?

Tune in to this now as a word or simply as a feeling and vibrational essence.

And in this simple act, you progress in more fully embodying the truth that you are.

Divine light from above flows down, down from the golden sun of light, in through your crown chakra, along your spinal column, down to the earth, where you are able to feel your connection with the earth and All That Is.

It flows back up, anchoring you to the light of the Divine above. It pours down, in through your crown chakra, along your spinal column, and out the bottom of your feet.

Circling back up, this divine light links you to the Divine and the heavens above, pouring down through your being towards the earth, and flowing back up towards the Divine.

This circular flow of energy, this divine tour of light flows in and around you, positively rippling out, assisting Gaia, Mother Earth, in returning to her authentic vibration and truth; assisting humanity, as one collective, in returning to an authentic vibration and truth; assisting individuals in returning to the heartfelt place of knowing and connection with the Divine, the heartfelt place of experiencing self.

Allow this energy to flow within and around you for as long as you like.

Stay in your authentic truth in this energy of divine love, knowing that being love, radiating light, being true to the authentic spiritual being that you are, is powerful work in and of itself.

In every moment, in any moment in which you return to this authentic vibration, you are positively contributing to the healing of the planet, to the healing of humanity, to the healing of self and of others.

The love vibration is a core aspect of your authentic truth; it is a core aspect of the authentic truth of all.

And so, returning to love, returning to this—your home vibration, which is love, which is high vibrational, which feels good, which cleanses you, which brings healing, which aligns you with your next steps in fully accomplishing your purpose—is powerful work indeed.

In this moment, in every moment, return to love.

Return to your home vibration and know that you are supported by the high vibrational guide, the ascended master who you have connected with today, who is not only your guide for today but always. You have their assistance, so remember to leverage it.

When you are in need of help, of restoring your diamond light body—your crystalline, high vibrational, authentic home vibration and state—shine the light that you are and progress one step at a time.

For now, we are complete.

And so, it is.

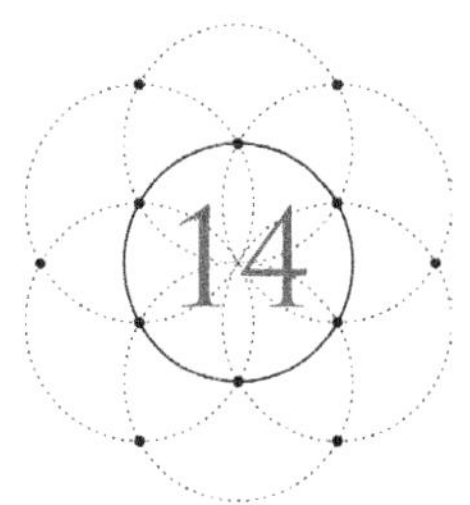

DIVINITY

We connect with you through frequency now, as love, light, and high vibrational energy from the spiritual realm enters into this time and space.

Pillars of light flow in and break up whatever cloud cover may be present, which is blocking you from experiencing the ultimate truth that is your direct connection with the Divine.

Light enters into this here and now.

And as you focus within, breathe and relax. You are able to experience lifting in vibration, as your physical body appears to become lighter in its form, as your emotional state of being is balanced and realigned with love, as your thoughts are elevated in vibration here and now.

Do not worry about lower vibrational thought or feeling that enters in, for you are not this.

You are not your thoughts.

You are not the sensations of your physical form.

You are not your emotions.

You are divine spirit. You are a part of the Creative Source essence.

Experience your oneness with the light of the Divine now. Allow your vibration to be lifted out of the density, out of duality to experience the underlying truth, and direct presence with God, Source, and All That Is.

For many, this is perceived as feeling light, as feeling bright. But ultimately, whatever you experience, it just *is*.

The intricacies of your physical expression are part of a convincing illusion.

The underlying truth is that you and everyone whom you encounter, everything you encounter in the physical world and in your inner world through thought, emotion, feeling, and sensation—everything you experience is unified, is God manifest, is Creative Source, who has shaped itself into you, into the physical world, into the people you encounter on your path.

Your mind may resist this concept. But for right now, just observe.

Step back and observe the truth of what is happening now, as you listen with your eyes closed and your heart open.

You are able to step back from the perspective of a physical being, a personality, and of having that be real. You are able to step back in perspective now with your eyes closed and your heart open to simply observe.

Observe what is appearing in your mind's eye. Observe what is appearing in your inner realm.

Is it thought, emotion, feeling, or sensation, a mental image, a movie playing before you, a song?

Observe, not judging what you perceive as good or bad, but letting it simply be.

In the same way, imagine observing what happens in your physical life around you—someone you meet, something that happens, something you see in life unfolding before you.

And you indeed have the ability to observe your life, the world around you, and the inner world within you from the same vantage point, from the same position of truth, from the perspective of infinite Creative Source—who, again, is not separate from you and did not create you to be here yet is in a separate location now, observing you from above.

What we are saying to you now is that Creative Source, God, created itself into you and into every aspect of your physical world.

And so, the concept of oneness is not awakening logically to experience some sort of energetic connection with everyone or everything in existence.

Truly awakening oneness is to experience and perceive all of life through the perspective of the observer—God, infinite Creative Source manifest as you, as the other people you encounter, as other people on the planet—people whom you consider to be good, people whom your mind would consider to be bad—as things you have grown to love, things your mind resists, and at a deep level, things you fear, judge, or even hate.

Beneath this story that plays out in the physical world, in the realm of duality, you are able to step back and simply observe everything that happens ... whether it appears internally—in this inner space, through thought, feeling, emotion, waveforms of energy in the void, which you are always able to tune in to by focusing within, becoming aware when thoughts arise and not being attached to them—or whether it is in the outer physical world, and the situations or challenges or dramas play out.

Ultimately, these are all infinite Creative Source manifest in an intricate, interwoven dance and story playing out, in which you are an important character.

You are ultimately a character because you and everyone else at the underlying level are part of the infinite Creative Source manifest in the hologram, paradigm, story, game, or experience.

Call and perceive it however you would like. Infinite Creative Source has molded itself into you and into everything—in all of existence on planet Earth, the Pleiades, the angelic realms, and beyond.

And so, this offers you deeper insight into how you are able to be one with a friend, a family member, an angel, an ascended master, or with us, the Council of Light, with a Pleiadian, a dog, a plant, or with planet Earth and beyond, continuing indefinitely.

Because everything that is, is united. Because everything that is—including the voice that speaks these words, the Council of Light that broadcasts this frequency and message, and you who listen and observe—is made up of and is infinite Creative Source, God, goddess, All That Is.

Pure source energy, the Divine, has created itself into physical form and into everything that is.

And we tell you this not to mess with you or to shake your value or worth. But we tell you, for with this perspective and knowing of truth, you are able to step back and simply observe in any moment.

Know that the true Creative Source has created and manifests everything, judges nothing, and simply observes the dance, the game, the story of life as it unfolds—the rich multidimensional, multimedia story, which you are a part of.

Infinite Creative Source has not created challenges or tragedies in your life or in the world to watch you go through them from an outside perspective.

Creative Source manifests itself as you, as the joy, the challenge, the bliss, and the experience that caused trauma, in order to experience itself as one with you, not separate.

Creative Source manifests as you in order to experience—

through your life—all the many facets of being alive in the realm of duality, of walking an ascension path, of walking a spiritual path in a seemingly dense, challenging, physical world.

And so, the blessing is that you are never separate from God and from the Divine, even when you are challenged.

All you have to do is realize and recognize this by stepping back to observe.

You are not your body. You are not your challenge. You are not your choice. You are not your blessing. You are not your bliss. You are not your life.

Observe from this outside perspective.

Step back and look through the window as Creative Source, as God, witnessing with non-judgment, with eternal love the story unfolding for you and your life, one moment at a time.

As you journey through life, experience what it would be like if Creative Source lived through you as a physical being disconnected from the absolute truth, but ultimately walking the path to reawaken, to remember, to realign and to now observe, as the story continues to unfold.

The awakening path and process of you, dear spiritual being, is divine Creative Source manifested through your body, mind, spirit, and life.

Step back into perspective.

Observe and allow what it is to be.

This is your reunion with that which has always been the underlying truth that God and infinite Source is manifest through you.

You do not make your heart beat. Your personality self does not make your lungs work. God, Creative Source is behind the entire illusion.

And by stepping back in perspective and opening your heart, you are able to, at multiple levels, feel, perceive, and observe this underlying truth.

At this time, you are lifted in light and love to further support you in stepping back, away from whatever dramas are playing out in your story.

Know that you are able to return to this place of observer time and time again, and at a deep level, that all is well, and that the Divine, God, Source, is manifest through you and through all.

15 YOUR INNER DIVINE BEING AWAKENING

We are here and we invite you in this moment to once again envision yourself in a circle with the masters, guides, and angels who serve and assist you from beyond the veil.

And so, let your hands reach out and take the hands of your beloved ones.

As you do, notice an immediate shift in your vibration as you are lifted in vibration to resonate with the purity and peace and light of these spiritual beings who are here to assist you in this moment now.

We assist you in stepping into your truth, for you are no less than, but you are equal to Masters in their highest vibrational state.

This state is what we are assisting you in reuniting with now, by flowing in plasma light of the divine, the crystalline liquid light that flows in all around you—bathing your body, mind, and spirit, elevating your vibration, and supporting you in fully being here now, fully present with your team of light who, together, create a golden circle of oneness.

And now, tune into the white light of purity spiraling in the center, flowing around in a divine spiral of tranquility from left to right.

As this light spirals, imagine that it begins to elevate, so that rather than simply spiraling horizontally, it begins to spiral vertically up, up into the light, rising up from the earth, to the sun, to the great central sun into oneness with Source, Light, All That Is.

Feel your same oneness with this as we now direct your attention to the space below your feet. Tune into that space, that void, that primordial force energy that begins to rise up.

You may envision this as golden light rising up through the bottom of your feet, up into your root, sacral, solar plexus. Breathe in, breathing light into your being. And as you exhale, imagine this light is being pulled upward, up into your heart, throat, third eye, crown, at the top of your head.

Breathe and focus your awareness at your crown chakra, breathing light into this center, activating your crown level vortex. And as you exhale, let this energy expand.

Breathe into your crown and as you exhale, let the thousand-petal lotus blossom wide. Your crown chakra opens to receive the transmission of pure Source presence available to you now to access and translate the infinite light of Source in this moment now.

Let your crown chakra open as you become aware of your flow of energy, the toroidal flow of your light body which extends up from your root in a column of light flowing up, uniting all of your chakras as one pillar of pure white light, fueling your crown chakra with the source light of your spine, flowing up into your crown and then spiraling out around you, filling your aura, your light body, your entire being with brilliant divine light.

Becoming aware of your spinal column completely glowing with crystalline light, imagine that this column is expanding outward, wider than your physical body, completely filling every cell with golden crystalline light, activating at the cellular level in every cell, your highest potential, your true divine nature at the cellular level.

Envision this column of light continuing to expand, encompassing your mental, emotional, auric, casual and spiritual being, recalibrating you at every level with the peace and serenity and tranquility and radiant possibility of your true divine nature.

You become aware now of this giant pillar of light around you encompassing your entire home, encompassing a vast area of space around you. It represents the ascension column of your higher divine being.

And so, expand in awareness to tune into your greater self, to tune into your authentic self, your divine self who is vast, powerful, radiant, and completely illuminated, completely shining with divine light.

Become aware of your heart chakra completely illuminated at the center of your physical being, your spiritual being, your divine being. Your heart center pulses with the light of the divine, creating ripples of divine authenticity out into the world around you.

Your heart chakra is now being recalibrated to your divine soul tone—your resonance—as you connect physically, mentally, emotionally, spiritually with Source, bringing your tone, your vibration, your authenticity in alignment with divine will ... with your highest, most authentic, most radiant possible expression.

And you simply bask in this unity now with your higher divine self, knowing that this is the first step in merging with your highest level of authenticity and with your higher levels of service—service through simply being, through embodying all that you are.

Service through receiving inspired intuition as to the inspired action you can take in the physical realm on the mental plane as a spiritual being to support the awakening collective.

For your being here now is no mistake; your connecting with your divine essence now is no mistake, for this is the paradigm all of humanity as a collective, as one, as a species, as individuals have the opportunity to transition into now.

Your experiencing this as an individual now paves the root for all.

And so, become aware of the ascension column of your higher divine self, the chakras of your highest self all united as one column of light that surrounds your entire being.

It fills your entire space with your authentic divine presence, bringing your entire space into harmony with your divine authenticity, paving the pathway before you and opening the doors of possibility for your highest vibrational manifestations, for you as a divine being to call in and forth the radiant possibility for your future as an individual, for your puzzle piece to be entirely illuminated, for your thread of the tapestry of collective consciousness to rise to a new level, for your contribution to the symphony that is the divine song you are partaking in.

Your piece is elevated in vibration, aligned with the highest authenticity, which cannot help but to realign and call forth the unification and divine resonance throughout all, coming into coherence with the source tone of perfection.

Become aware of the most beautiful tone or sound that you can imagine.

This inner sound therapy soothes you on every level. It brings your every cell into vibrational alignment with Source, and supports you in expanding, in opening, in elevating to tune into the vast realm beyond the physical, the vast realm of Source and Spirit available to you.

You are enabled to explore and to experience the

miraculous possibility and vastness of this source field of the infinite that you are a part of.

By tuning into Source in this way—by expanding and lifting and opening and diving in—you are able to now call forth the blessings of the divine into your life, the opportunities in alignment with your highest interest and the highest interest of all.

The fresh new perspectives, the vibrant new level of radiance and well-being are downloaded now into your awareness, into your mental, physical, spiritual, auric being.

Receive these downloads like a waterfall of light pouring down upon you, revitalizing and reconnecting you with the joy and magic of co-creating with the infinite ... in alignment, in resonance, in perfect harmony with your soul tone and your highest level of divine authenticity.

Open your heart, tuning into the light within your heart glowing brightly, letting this light expand around you.

Now, tune into the heart light that is all around you, the love vibration surrounding you at every level. Bask in this love, lift in this love, and know that you are this love vibration.

And so, let yourself release for just a moment the perspective of yourself as a physical being and tune into the infinite love of the vast source field that you are a part of. Expand, breathe, and know that the particles of

Source are rearranging and rewriting the possibilities for your future.

A timeline and paradigm does indeed exist for your most radiant, most joyful, most rewarding, highest service, incredibly loving radiant life.

And in this moment—your heart open, your ascension column illuminated, your crown blossoming and receiving the infinite light—you are aligned with this highest paradigm.

It is love that aligns you with the infinite light available to call forth into being ... to not only experience on an abstract or meditative level, but to write with light, to create with love and light of spirit into tangible physical form, to transform the paradigm in which you live, the earth that you are a part of, the humanity that you are one with, to ascend and step into this new level of radiant living and vibrant love and light.

You are supported by the team of Guides and Angels and Ascended Masters who surround you.

We take your hands, creating this circle of light, to support you in ushering in the vibrant possibilities available for your life. We bring to your awareness now the area where you are already shining the most light in your life.

What are you already doing to shine light in the world?

What are the little things and actions you do, creating ripples of light and positivity and love throughout creation?

And now, what new action or state of being or pattern or level of service is available for you to step into, to contribute love and light on an even greater scale?

You will receive the vibrational resonance of this now. You may receive a specific, visual, inspired action or possibility or you may not, but you are vibrationally aligning with this next level of your highest service.

The way is being paved, the door is being opened, your team of guides and angels and masters are guiding you in this direction through your intuition, through synchronicity, through signs, through joy.

Follow the path of joy and love.

Follow the radiant, vibrant, exciting path of bliss to serve, love, make a difference, and merge with your higher divine self on a new level.

Taking a large leap up the staircase of light into embodying more of the divine light being you authentically are—becoming aware of your circle of mastery, your circle of golden light, holding hands with your team—now become aware of this circle intersecting with all other awakened beings on the planet, surrounding the earth with the divine geometry of light.

Receive the love and light available to you now and share this forth towards all ... to receive love, give love, and restore the harmony and radiance of divinely inspired living.

Receive the blessings of light and love and shine these

forth around the entire planet—light filling the entire earth, restoring the divine soul tone of Gaia, Mother Earth, the vibrational energetic signature of the earth that is in alignment with the highest divine possibility, that is in union with the Divine Source song.

You are a part of this realignment and we will continue to support you as you walk this path of radiant love into the highest possible future, in alignment with divine will and the highest interest of all.

We leave you now with our love, light and blessing.

Receive the love at the cellular level; receive the light at the level of your soul; integrate from soul to cell to embody the divine light, to live as the divinely awakened being you are.

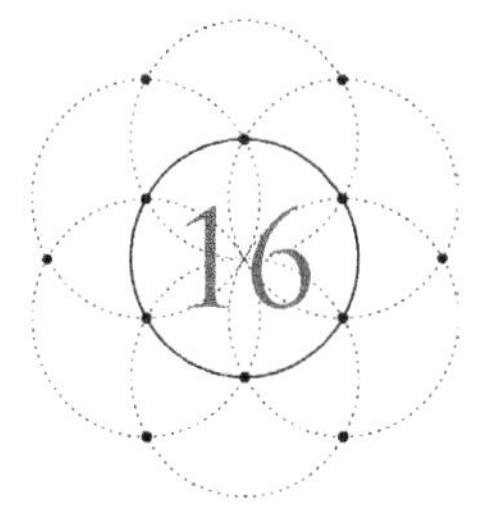

RETURN TO YOUR AUTHENTIC VIBRATION

We greet you in this moment with an immense supply of love, of peace, and of tranquility. We energetically assist you now in letting go of what has been, in letting go of thought and focusing on the outside world around you, in letting go and entering within.

Let your mind become still and calm.

Let your heart open wide.

Focus within, breathe, and go inward.

We are pleased to assist you in tuning into the truth of your authentic vibration, to the truth of the vibration of your spiritual self, of your authentic self, of the fullness that you are as a multidimensional spiritual being in physical form.

By tuning into this truth of your authentic self, you can return, maintain, live in alignment with this, your authentic home vibration, your inner truth, your energetic signature that is called for at this time on earth.

It has a key role to play in the unfolding ascension and evolution of the collective consciousness and earth, which you are a part of, which you are one with.

Your unique energetic signature is necessary to usher in positive change, to bring the oneness and divine love to the forefront of consciousness for all humanity, to bring a great flow of ascension energy, which will carry you, your earth, and all of humanity further into your becoming, further into being in alignment with divine will, with your highest possible potential, and indeed, with love, well-being, positive co-creation, and positive change.

This authentic vibration and truth that you are in spirit, that you were before being birthed into the physical realm, is available for you to return to always.

Your very vibration and the understanding and knowing of what this is, is a tool.

For yes, there will be times when the energy of another, unconsciously, has an adverse impact on your own.

You may absorb some sort of density.

You may become shaken by an outside event.

You may get caught up in chaos or struggle or the energies of doubt, and you can then catch the shift in your energy. You can catch and become aware that your vibrational level has dropped, that you are in a lower vibrational state.

But no matter what the reason for your energetic shift, for your drop in vibration, with awareness, you can consciously choose to shift back, to enter within and return to your authentic vibration, your home vibration, to the vibration of the spiritual being that you authentically are.

It is, by default, high vibrational. And by default, it overflows through and beyond you in alignment with love, compassion, and joy, in accordance with divine will, infused with light to positively impact all.

And so, at this time, focus within.

Focus on your heart and imagine you are diving into it, going within and allowing your heart to open.

Tune into your energy. Tune into your body.

Breathe and pay attention to how you feel as you breathe in wellness and vitality, and as you exhale anything that is not your authentic truth.

Don't worry about what your authentic vibration is. At this time, just tune into how you are feeling right now, knowing that you are surrounded with light, and you're safe to simply be, to breathe, to focus within, and to let go.

Tune into how you feel.

Are there worries or concerns that started off as thoughts and are now energetic frequencies in your aura and your personal energetic signature?

Are there areas of pain, of physical discomfort, which again started off as thought in one form or another and have now manifested physically as a calling card, drawing your awareness to an imbalance and a need to return to the energetic signature, which is authentically yours?

Become aware of your energy now, as you continue to breathe and relax, as you are soothed, nurtured, and calmed by your team of guides and angels who are here with you now to support you in entering in, to support you in returning home to the vibration, to the frequency, to the light that is your authentic truth, that is the presence and energy of your higher self.

At this time, know that you are in the presence of many guides and angels who serve you according to divine will, who stand firmly in the light and support you from behind the scenes.

Know that you are protected, you are loved, and you are able to let go.

Focus within.

And now, at this time, imagine and become aware of the vibration of your higher self, manifesting as a light being here and now, coming into this present time and space, standing behind you.

Envision an orb of diamond white light above your head, which lowers down in this light being that is your higher self, embodying your authentic vibration, embodying the diamond light body, which is standing behind you now.

Your higher self, completely connected with your authentic truth, is unhindered by any blockage, by any energy belonging to another, by any negativity or density or vibration, which is not love and which is not true to your authentic being, your purpose, your frequency, your light as a spiritual being in physical form.

It spans multidimensions and many lines of time, but is present here and now, and ready to align with the truth of all that you are at this time; your higher self, embodying the diamond light body standing behind you now, places their hands upon your shoulders.

Feel the shift in your energy.

Your energetic signature now begins to take on the qualities of your authentic truth.

Your energetic signature is cleansed and purified and uplifted to match the vibration of your higher self, present here and now in a diamond light body standing behind you with hands on your shoulders, assisting you in returning to the knowing of your authentic energy signature.

Your home vibration, the truth of who you are as a light being, as a spiritual being in physical form, embodies this authentic spirit now.

Your higher self is standing behind you, your guides and angels all around, assisting in this process ... and now, experience and imagine the diamond light body of your higher self, merging with you.

Imagine the mind of your higher self uniting with your mind, the hands of the diamond light body becoming one with your hands, the organs of the diamond light body completely healthy, vital and energized, uniting with your organs.

Picture the skin of your divine light body uniting with your physical skin ... the cells, the vibrant, awakened cells united with the divine light body of your higher self now merge with your cells in your physical being.

The diamond light body of your higher self merges with your physical body: the spirit merging with your spirit, the mind merging with your mind; the mind, body, spirit of your higher self merges with you now.

And as this happens, any blockages that were stored within your physical body, within your spirit, within your mind are released, are pushed out, for light and dense energy cannot occupy the same space.

And just as a candle lit in a dark room dispels the darkness, so too does the entrance of your light, the entrance of your higher self and light body into your physical being now release and dissolve and disperse all density, all blockages, all attachments, all energy of others, all that is not yours.

All that is not love, all that is not in alignment with your authentic truth and home vibration releases into the light now.

We give you a moment now to just be.

Breathe and experience and bask in this light of your home vibration. You may feel it as joy or love or compassion or serenity or peace.

Notice what you feel.

Become aware of what you sense.

Experience the truth of your authentic energetic signature as you let go of all you are not to tune into the truth of that which you authentically are, a spiritual light being, vibrating in physical form, present in physical form here and now.

Breathe and tune into your authentic vibration. Open your heart and experience.

Experience your home vibration coming in more fully and more completely. As you open your heart, let go and enter into the still, calm, and yet vibrantly alive presence of your light found within.

We now offer you the metaphor of a tuning fork, played amidst the frequency contained within, far and wide. And so, your team of guides and guardian angels now ping your energy, your authentic vibration.

Like a sonic boom, an explosion of love and light, your authentic vibration sweeps across existence, flowing out from you, overflowing out from you and to all, filling the room you are in, the continent you are on, the planet you are on with your authentic vibration and essential role in the greater energy of one, making up all that is.

And as your energy flows out beyond you, notice the

lights it encounters.

Notice meeting the other souls who are standing in their authentic light and vibration, the other people on the planet who are in alignment with their authentic truth, who are present in this moment or in any moment, for time is not linear.

Notice those who are standing in their home vibration, in the vibration aligned with the truth of their higher self, light being, and soul.

As your energy flows out, notice these lights and notice that just by being true to your authentic light, to your authentic vibration, that just by being and radiating these qualities of the Divine that you embody, you are making a difference.

You are accelerating the ascension.

You are serving to awaken others, serving to assist others in releasing old energies of pain and control and returning to their authentic truth, centered in love, found within, through the open heart, quiet mind, and awakened spiritual light.

Become aware of your diamond light body, one and united with your physical form.

Open your heart and imagine a diamond of light brightly shining within.

Imagine perceiving reality through the lens of love,

perceiving reality through the vantage point of your heart, in alignment with compassion for all, for self, in alignment with love.

And now, imagine this diamond in your mind receiving clarity of light, clarity of purpose, receiving the mental knowledge of when you are in your authentic vibration, so you can consciously know when you are not.

When your vibration has dropped and when you need to complete this exercise, once more, of going within, all you do is open your heart and allow the diamond light body of your higher self, that is you authentically in spirit, to return, to reunite, to merge, and to become one with your physical body, your mental body, and your spiritual body in this or in any moment.

If you were to now think of all that is wrong in the world, if you were to now think of the things that are challenging you in your life, if you were to now think of hardship and struggle and suffering, if you were to now even listen to these words and tune in to this heavier vibration, you would slightly, you will, you did slightly shift in vibration away from your authentic truth, away from your authentic energy signature.

But the good news is you can quickly shift back.

And so, just as easy as it was to drop slightly in vibration on hearing the word *suffering* or *pain*, you can now lift in vibration, return to your authentic truth, return to your home vibration by opening your heart, entering in, and thinking of love, thinking of love for yourself, thinking of love for all ... thinking, feeling, and tuning into your diamond light body and to the presence of your higher self as easily as it is to drop in frequency, to fall into a lower vibration.

So, too, it is that easy to shift when you quiet your mind. For your mind is the biggest obstacle in this.

And so, quiet your mind, open your heart, tune into the vibration of love, and shift back into the full embodiment of your authentic vibration, of your diamond light body, being the present enlightened spiritual being that you are, here and now, aware of and radiating this immense light that is unique to you, that is beautiful, that is authentically who you are.

When you return to this vibration, healing occurs and clarity unfolds.

A fuller alignment with your purpose and knowing of your next steps naturally occurs.

Certain technologies and movies and media and ads have a knack for shifting you out of your home vibration. Become aware in the moment and enter in, just as you have done today, to tune into how you feel, to how you are vibrating energetically.

And if you are not in alignment with the authentic light and spirit that you are, shift, open your heart, quiet your mind, invite in the presence of your diamond light body.

Invite in the presence of divine love, and shine as the divine spiritual being that you are, as the light being that you are, as the powerful, creative, beautiful, magnificent, unlimited spiritual being here in a physical form, here to serve, to love, to grow, to make a difference.

You are here to continue to progress on your individual and collective ascension path, bringing about immense positive change in your life and on a grand scale for the entire planet, for all of humanity, one moment and one step at a time, returning home to your authentic truth and to your personal authentic, light-filled, high vibrational energetic signature.

Breathe and tune into the truth of your authentic vibration once more.

Enjoy, radiate, bask in this light.

And once more, feel your vibration of love, of divine presence, centered in your heart and now flowing outward—a simple, subtle, profound blessing flowing out towards all, spanning vast distances across the lines of time.

Standing in your truth, embodying your authentic self, brings healing to your family, to your friends, to those whom you know and those whom you do not. For standing in your authentic truth paves the pathway for another to do the same.

And now, tune into the visualization of bright lights

covering the entire planet of all of humanity, standing true to the light beings that you all authentically are.

Know that your work here and your presence, your simply *being* is bringing this potential future closer into being.

As a collective, you are making progress in this direction.

As an individual, you can make a difference.

In the moment, return to love. Return to the authentic truth that you are ... and from this knowing and from this presence, act accordingly.

Experience your home vibration coming in more fully and more completely. As you open your heart, let go and enter into the still, calm, and yet vibrantly alive presence of your light found within.

17 GOLDEN CRYSTALLINE LIGHT ACTIVATION

Indeed, we are present here and now and we invite you to begin to relax so that you can, from a relaxed and inward focused place of being, tune into our presence through your subtle inner senses.

Tune into our message. Tune into the frequency, light, and love we broadcast now.

And so, get comfortable, breathe, and let go.

Enter inward.

Relax as you now begin to imagine and tune into golden plasma light that, like liquid, begins to fill the room or space you are in, flowing in around your feet. This golden liquid light flows all around your feet and, indeed, flows into every cell.

And so, within your feet and around this area, tune into the golden light, the golden crystalline light that begins to rise, filling your space, filling this present point in time, streaming in through the great central sun, through your sun, moon, and to your planet ... flowing into your present point in time, up, covering your feet, filling the space like liquid light flowing up along your legs, up to cover your knees.

Feel the light flowing within your legs and around.

As the level of light continues to rise, a warm, tingling, high vibrational energy relaxes and reconnects you with the infinite. As the level of light continues to rise, let it flow into your thighs and hips, filling your entire legs, your abdomen, your pelvic area, and filling the room you are in.

Like water rising, this liquid continues to flow up into your abdomen, your solar plexus, and your heart. The liquid light flows into your fingers, wrists and arms, your elbows, shoulders and neck. It flows into your high heart, your chest, flowing in and all around.

Experience the light filling your physical body, raising your rate of vibration, relaxing you at a profoundly deep level.

Feel the light within … and now, tune into the vast flow of liquid golden light that is all around, that now continues to rise up through your throat, your jaw, your ears, up into your head, filling your mind, your eyes, your third eye and your crown, filling your hair with light, filling your entire head with the golden crystalline light.

Tune into this light at the center of your mind brightly shining, filling every cell, raising your vibration from within, soothing, calming, uplifting.

And now, tune into the light that is all around you, the light that is above your head and extending out in every direction. Feel the light behind you, illuminating you from all around, this liquid crystalline light that you are completely immersed in.

And now, as the level of light rises exponentially, imagine that you are being lifted up in it, lifted up into a special place outside of time, lifted up into a circle of masters, a circle of your team of soul family and guides and loved ones beyond the veil, the team of masters who guide and support you with their full divinity and light intact.

We as the Council of Light join this circle as well—your guides in this moment now holding hands, immersed in this golden crystalline plasma light.

Feel your hands light up as the link of this circle is complete with your joining in.

At the center of this vast circle, you become aware of a spiral of white light—the white light of purity at the center of this circle flowing in a spiral of light, in a clockwise direction from your left hand around and into your right, flowing with divine purity, tranquility, serenity and peace.

And as you hold this circle, now become aware of the many other awakened human beings on the planet, each in their own circle of light, their circle of mastery reunited with their guides and their divinity.

Become aware of each of your circles overlapping to create first a vesica piscis as you unite with one other circle and then a triad and then a seed of life and then a flower of life.

This flower of life—your circle, a small part, but an

integral part in this divine geometric form—spans out far and wide to encompass the entire earth.

And so, imagine Gaia, Mother Earth, with the flower of life imprinted upon her surface, the golden outline with the white light of purity within. And now, imagine that this flower of life is expanding.

It is elevating in vibration and extending out beyond into the cosmos, expanding out across the solar system, across the Milky Way galaxy.

You may envision the sun with this same flower of life pattern around it. And from the earth to the sun, to the great central sun with this flower of life geometry, you are now connected to the golden arc.

This allows you as a divine being to receive directly from Source—through the great central sun—the light codes, the awakened frequency, the activation available to you now.

You are, in a sense, revealing more of your authentic divine nature as you link through this golden arc through the sacred geometric bridge with the highest levels of light and with the divine authenticity that is available for you now to embody.

You may now imagine yourself as an individual standing upon the earth, your arms stretched out as you are bathed in a waterfall, a beam of plasma golden light that is crystalline in nature and that raises your vibration, flowing up and arcing out, so that you are standing in the midst of a funnel.

Imagine yourself reaching up and out to receive all that is available to you now as a divine human, as an ascending being, as a divine spiritual being in physical form who is now claiming your empowerment and your true divine sovereign nature to refill your light quotient, to renew your vitality, to directly reconnect with the infinite source light that you are a part of and that flows through the divine geometry of creation through the primordial sound throughout all.

Become aware now of your heart glowing with this golden plasma light, expanding out beyond your physical body and beyond your aura.

Your heart light expands out to fuel your light body, to reconnect you with the fullness of your light as a spiritual being. Let your heart expand as you relax and remain focused within, just basking in this frequency flowing all around you, basking in the infinite love, the purity, harmony and possibility as you are in this moment transformed through your expansion and direct reconnection with the infinite source light.

The golden plasma crystalline light, flowing all around you, supercharges your vibration and revitalizes you on every level.

Become aware of the new level of light you carry within by focusing on the light and space and vastness within you.

Breathe and expand into it.

Open up to the magnificence and the miracle of your inner light being.

And now, tune into the light, the crystalline consciousness, the vastness of void and space that is all around you. Focusing on the space around your being extending out infinitely from this present point in time, feel your connection and oneness with this vastness ... for this, too, you are a part of.

Feel the light, the liquid light of the divine all around you, within you; become aware once more of yourself in the circle with your team and guides of light serving as an anchor of the higher vibration on the earth, serving as a light being, calling forth the paradigm of peace and joy and awakened creativity.

Become aware of your circle and the vast flower of life you are creating that now clicks into place around the earth and links into the crystalline grid, so that around the planet, the light of the crystalline grid, the light of the awakened earth, the new earth, the new paradigm, the peace and joy and positivity and opportunity is made manifest, is accessed, is revealed.

Open your heart and let love and joy and vibrant energy flow forth towards all who make up this human heart grid, towards all who make up this flower of divine life.

And as you freely share your love and gratitude, your light, as you freely share the codes of awakening and ascension frequencies you have integrated and can therefore shine forth, you then receive the blessing of this transmission multiplied.

Your willingness to share and serve with love opens the doors to your heart even wider and you now receive the fullness of the love, of the possibility and harmony available now.

Feel how vast you really are as a divine being awakening to a new level in the physical, restoring the possibility for this earthly realm to transform in the most beautiful way.

And now, with light all around you and with light within you, plant your feet squarely on the ground, anchoring this light of divine purity of the white and golden rays into your present point in time to bring these ascended streams of consciousness into your awareness not only in this moment and through meditation, but in every moment.

Thus, when you enter into your heart, you can access this vastness and this pure potentiality of your true power as a divine being in spiritual form.

And with this newly reconnected level of your light through the white and golden ray, through the crystalline plasma light, we encourage and remind you that your inspiration, your divine creativity, and your presence will continue to be your guide.

Return to presence, to inner stillness, radiantly shining your light.

Through this, the next step and the way before you into the next level, into a new opportunity, a new possibility becomes available.

Keep your heart open.

Shine your radiant light.

And when you are ready, now return your awareness to your physical body, completely replenished, completely new, blessed, and realigned, knowing that you have done powerful work … and yet, the path of your highest divine authenticity is simply beginning.

Inspiration leads to your next step on the pathway of infinite possibility into the full realignment on the level of mind, body, spirit, emotions with the highest level of your divine light bringing your full spiritual power into the physical, into one present moment at a time, a continued joy which creates a powerful ripple of crystalline consciousness through all.

As we step back, we flow a final surge of frequency and blessing your way.

Open your heart and let it in.

And so, it is…

18 LOVE AND LIGHT DNA ACTIVATION

We serve now to assist humanity and earth along the ascension timelines in becoming awakened Christ lights, fully activated ascended beings.

And we are pleased to assist with this activation while emphasizing that your ultimate ascension—becoming radiant Christ light—is your opportunity, your birthright to be chosen in the moment through embodying, vibrating, and ever ascending into greater levels of love and light.

As you commit to this path of letting go of all that is lower vibrational—based in fear, illusion, and tension, as well as drama and negativity—you are able to ascend. Recognize that these things of lower vibrations are not bad, for this is judgment, what you are learning to rise above.

Rather, shift from judgment into discernment away from good and bad and ask:

Is this for my highest and greatest?

Is this not in alignment with my highest or is this neutral?

Do you see the difference?

Returning to love and light is what ushers your ascension

further. So, progress in this direction every moment and join us now in experiencing a leap through an activation empowered by the highest levels of love and light that you may perceive as streaming in all around you, from above, below, behind, and beside.

But know that, ultimately, this same love and light are already accessible within. And to fully tune into this love and light, this Divine Source light available now to accelerate your ascension and activate your multidimensional crystalline DNA, you must go within.

For this cannot be accessed through the outside world or the ego mind on the linear timeline.

This truth, light, and vibrant radiance can only be sensed and tuned into from within.

At this time, relax and let go of the focus on the outside world around you. Relax and enter inward, focusing your awareness in the center of your chest, in the center of your spinal column where you tune into your heart light.

Let the light build and accumulate herein.

We surround you in a circle of love and light with each of our hearts open, broadcasting love, ascension keys, and codes of consciousness, multidimensional truth your way in the form of pure light, sunlight, source light, and self-love light.

Open your heart to tune into the light, to let your heart build and grow with the most vibrant light you can imagine.

And extending beyond that, let your heart chakra—your heart center, your portal to your multidimensional truth, the gateway to ascension that you carry within—fill with infinite light and love, with Source presence.

As it fills your heart, expanding out beyond your physical body, your aura, your room, and your home, you are shining with your heart center as bright as a star in the greater multidimensional galaxy.

Let your brilliance shine.

Let go of past beliefs of smallness, and let go of anything that is lower and not serving in vibration with your highest truth.

Your soul light is vibrantly shining from within your heart, filling every inch of your body, your emotions, mind, spirit; love and light shine within and all around you. You are so supported, safe, loved, and encouraged.

Release fear and density; embrace love and light.

In the spirit, the starlight that you are and carry within, we are honored to serve you in rekindling now.

Let your heart light shine into every cell of your physical body, filling and radiating every cell with the highest vibrational light, pure sunlight, source light, Christ light, and multidimensional crystalline light.

Zoom in with your awareness, with your focus on a cell that is past the tipping point and fully light.

Now from Source light, we call upon DNA activation within all your cells, so all 12 strands of your DNA are activated with the highest light that is streaming to your planet in an abundant supply, just waiting for you to choose and accept.

Think or say and repeat, *I activate my DNA now with love and light.* Thus all 12 strands of your DNA are healed, restored, balanced, and activated.

Now the 13th-strand DNA activation downloads into your DNA; the pure Christ strand of DNA, Christ consciousness, divine, feminine, awakened multidimensional self downloads. And the 14th multidimensional strand direct from source downloads now.

Your DNA is downloaded with crystalline light and love to activate your multidimensional senses, gifts, abilities, and opportunities, as well as the new timelines available to you as a multidimensional being on Gaia, Mother Earth.

Open your heart and let yourself vibrantly shine with this new level of light activated. Choose to ascend into your highest truth.

And from the area of your heart, vibrantly glowing like the sun, imagine yourself linking to the collective network of humanity, sharing these activated codes of DNA, ascension, multidimensional truth, and awakening with the greater fields of collective consciousness.

Indeed, all this light, the very essence of this activation, this highest vibrational essence of your truth as a divine being—which is the truth of divinity of all human beings—can be accessed and is here waiting for all to tune into the pathway paved with ascension and awakening.

Through your choice in this moment, allow your heart to glow vibrantly, filled with the light of Source, the starlight and sunshine light that you are.

And in this place, become aware of Gaia transforming the same way the heart of Gaia, the heart of Mother Earth, shining as bright as the sun.

Mother Earth, too, is undergoing her ascension and becoming more star-like to pave the way for the new paradigm and new earth, for all humanity, to lay the new timelines of awakened living and being, expressing and loving.

Feel your oneness with the light of Gaia, the light of Mother Earth.

Feel your oneness with the light of Source, the light of the Divine.

Feel your oneness with the light brightly shining within your heart, the light all around you, the light of love.

Feel, shine with, and embody this vibrant starlight, awakened Christ being, and know that each time you return to this process of calling forth the activation of your DNA, the light and love within you, your progression will continue.

As this path of your ascension that is your choosing continues to unfold, to bring forth your high vibrational, multidimensional crystalline timeline of beauty, it rewrites the paradigm for your life and for earth with the love and light that you are, which you brightly carry and shine as a star from within.

We are honored to support you any time you wish to repeat this process.

Enter inward, let light shine in your heart, and activate the highest truth of that which you are.

And so, it is...

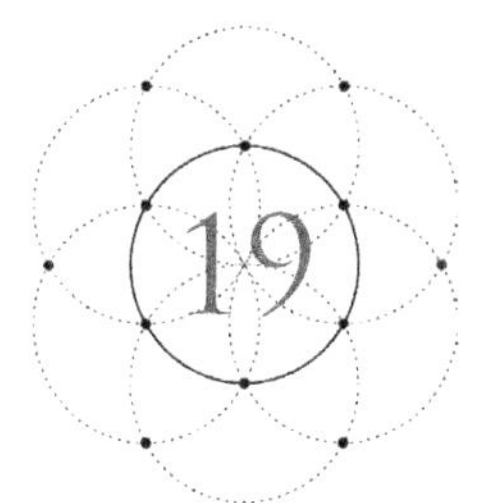

EMBODYING YOUR DIAMOND LIGHT BODY

Indeed, we, in conjunction with your team, surround you in a circle of love, flowing the qualities of divine love and light and presence around you.

You are safe and supported in letting go of focus upon the external and entering now into your inner state of being.

Open your heart and enter into the inner realm of your imagination and intuition.

Enter into a deeper state of mind.

Enter into your heart as your vibration now lifts to meet the higher dimensional light that is streaming in.

And so, the diamond light ray is shining down upon you and you are vibrationally lifting through this heart-centered place to meet it. Tune into the space of your open heart, tuning into diamond light therein. It is as if a diamond is glowing inside the center of your being, a diamond fully illuminated with divine, Christ, awakened, infinite light.

The diamond light of Spirit and of the infinite glow within

you. Focus all your awareness and your attention on this diamond light in your heart center.

Dive into it, experiencing the light glowing inside your heart, expanding to flow through your entire body, expanding down from your heart, into your lower energy centers, down through your legs and feet, extending out into your arms and hands, extending up into your neck and shoulders and mind.

The diamond light of your heart flows through your entire body.

As you breathe in, now imagine your heart light glowing brighter with diamond light. And on your exhale, envision the light flowing into every cell.

Every cell within your physical body is elevated in vibration and infused with this diamond light, elevating your vibration as a physical being into alignment with your diamond and crystalline blueprint, the blueprint for your divine perfection within physicality.

Tune into the light in your heart, the light in your physical body … and now, envision this diamond light expanding in an orb around you.

Tune into the diamond light all around your body, around your head, around your shoulders, in front of your chest, in back of your being, below your feet, around your legs, within and all around your physical body.

Let your awareness now be on this orb of diamond light

surrounding you as your vibration is further elevated with assistance from the divine and from all the beings of your team in the realm of Spirit who step forward, so that you can now lift.

And as you lift up on this diamond ray of light, the beings of the seraphim, the seraphim angels lower down to meet you. Imagine that you are now surrounded with the most vibrant, highest vibrational angels you have ever seen or perceived.

Their huge wings and glowing hearts surround you, raising your vibration even more, transferring the diamond heart light from their blueprint into yours, purifying your heart center and opening it to a new level, opening the pathway to the angelic realm and beyond, opening the doorway to direct oneness and unity with Spirit, God, with the infinite.

Tune into the diamond light all around you, becoming aware of a sense of floating up, lifting up and expanding out as you vibrationally elevate to embody more and more of the diamond light that is streaming onto the planet.

Open your heart to greet it.

Breathe and relax to allow it to flow throughout your entire physical form, to merge with your mind, to elevate your spirit, to soothe past emotional tensions and burdens.

Allow it to bring every aspect of your being into alignment with your highest interest, the highest level of integrity and the highest vibrational quality of light and energy available to you now.

Lift in the light that is all around you.

Lift on the six wings of each of the seraphim angels who surround you, who now lift you up further, lifting you up so that the exterior barrier of where your physical body ends and where the infinite begins seems to melt away, so that you can in this moment, simply experience yourself as one with the very seraphim on whose wings you lift.

Experience yourself as one with us, the Council of Light, with the diamond light, with the Divine, with the space all around you, with the light of the infinite, with the energy of creation and the space of the void, with divine masculine and feminine, with humanity, earth, angels, spiritual beings and all—experiencing the balance, the vastness, the complexity and simplicity of your oneness, your unity, and your direct link with the Divine.

And now, once again, focus your awareness inside of your heart center.

The diamond light in your heart now glows more vibrantly than ever before, elevating in vibration.

It is as if you carry a light brighter than the sun in your center, glowing with the purity of all of the rays of creation elevated into their highest vibrational state, in complete harmony and authenticity with the divine connection, in complete purity, balance, and oneness with Source.

Tune into this heart light.

Let it expand out, filling your physical body, cleansing away illusion and restoring the divine blueprint for your diamond light body manifest in your physical form, restoring the divine blueprint for your fulfillment, your joy, your abundance, your love.

Feel your power returned and restored in this present moment.

Tune into an area of your life where you have felt challenged as the diamond light resolves, heals, replenishes the divine authenticity and perfection in every way, so that you are able to see the underlying blessings of your challenge and see that you are now able to shift.

Your awareness is now drawn to a new chapter, a new possibility for your life, a vision for living in harmony with the divine, acting in alignment with the highest interest of all beings and stepping up and stepping forward to live as and to fully embody the diamond light being that you are.

Catch a glimpse of this vision for your future, the full potential of your radiance that is yet to be.

Catch a glimpse and now imagine that the diamond light from your heart is pouring forth, is flowing out in a spiral of divine perfection, in a spiral of sacred geometric form, surrounding your future with the same diamond light, strengthening the divine blueprint and bringing the 9th-dimensional qualities of divine perfection, of the diamond light blueprint, of your highest calling ... aligning this with your future, infused with your diamond heart light.

And now, like a puzzle finally being completed, the last piece, the last strands of light are clicked into place, aligning you in this present moment with the timeline of your highest integrity, your highest authenticity with the 9th-dimensional divine blueprint of crystalline creation and diamond light manifestation.

Your heart light flows forth beyond you, paving the pathway into your future, illuminating the opportunities in alignment with your highest interest and rinsing away what no longer serves you.

And so, as you, moving forward from this session, step forward into your new life, into your new future, be willing to change and to adapt, for you are stepping into a higher dimensional paradigm of experience.

Perhaps the intentions and manifestations you have been working on still apply, but perhaps, there is an even greater calling urging you forward.

Be open to all that this path has to reveal to you, letting go of being locked in, and instead going with the flow with ease and grace and tranquility, flowing in alignment with your highest truth.

And your heart, your heart filled with the diamond light, will keep you on course and on track.

Let your heart lead, keeping your heart light turned on and in the moment, being present, recognizing that from the place of presence is where opportunity appears.

And one step at a time, allow yourself to progress on this path of divine authenticity, of inspired being, of living as the embodied diamond light being in physical form.

At this time, the full blueprint of your diamond, crystalline higher self steps forward, lowers down, merges with you from all around, from every direction beyond space and time, above and below, behind, beside, from every direction and every dimension.

The diamond light quality and blueprint of your higher self steps forward.

Open your heart.

Open your heart and think *yes* to allow this integration with your highest self, with the highest possibilities for your life, with this opportunity to embody the fullness of the diamond light being you authentically are in spirit—which you are invited to now embody in physical form, bringing a greater spiritual quality to every aspect of your life, supercharging your manifestation ability and uniting you with the many blessings that are yet in store

Surrender the outcome and trust that, in this moment, you are fully aligned.

What is your next step in progressing on this path of your highest authenticity?

Let your heart light expand around you.

Infuse your home and your reality and your relationships

and your aspirations and your opportunities and your career and your hobbies and your passions with love, bringing every aspect of your life into sync ... bringing your body, mind, and spirit and every aspect of your reality into coherence with your highest divine authenticity, with the diamond light, with the blueprint for your divine perfection, balance, harmony, and inspiration.

With your heart light continuing to glow, your body tingling from this connection with Divine Presence and tingling from merging with your higher self, let your awareness now return to your physical body.

Find that it is now completely renewed, centered on a new timeline, in sync with your highest integrity and highest authenticity.

Return to your new life: a new reality refreshed, embodied, revitalized.

Let yourself now emerge from this meditative state, continuing to shine the diamond light within your heart that creates powerful ripples all around you, bringing this higher, finer, more vibrant quality of being into form, in a way that can be accessed by all.

Imagine that with your heart open, you're now contributing light forth towards humanity, towards peace on earth, towards infinite abundance, towards well-being of all, love, the highest interest of all.

Flowing light forth from your heart to the human heart

grid, become aware of your connection to this human heart grid, the diamond crystalline light surrounding the entire globe, ushering in the full embodiment of the new earth, the full embodiment of the highest paradigm that you are a part of, which you are calling forth, which serves you and ultimately serves all.

Keep your heart open. Keep shining this—your diamond radiant light—and know that you are so loved and supported as you simply continue to walk your path, to take your steps, to shine your light, to live in love and joy and peace and bliss and truth.

We love you, we bless you, we honor you and we flow a final surge of peace and tranquility, a blessing of serenity and illumination your way.

We are the Council of Light and we humbly serve you as you step forward into alignment with all that you authentically are.

Lift, shine, love, light up, expand.

And now, return to your new life, to your new body, to your reality, completely renewed and realigned with your highest interest.

And so, it is…

20 YOUR HIGHEST AUTHENTICITY

As you now allow yourself to relax and let go and enter into your inner realm, you are able to begin to perceive and experience our presence with your subtle senses.

As you relax, you bring yourself into our harmonic state of resonance in which you are able to receive the blessings of your highest authenticity, the reunion through conscious awareness as a physical being with your higher multidimensional selves.

You begin to experience the higher faculties of your light and the gifts and inspirations and creative nudges that align you as a physical being with your highest purpose and authenticity as a volunteer soul here in the physical, as an earth angel, a light worker, a divine being in physical form.

You are here, yes, to enjoy and love and learn and live and thrive, but you are also here to empower, inspire, serve with love, guide, and assist the collective consciousness of humanity at this paramount point in space and time in which new frontiers and opportunities, new ways of being are coming online—new archetypes, new creation frameworks for co-creation, vibrant well-being, harmony, and creativity.

You are able to pave the pathway into this new frontier by consciously choosing and being willing to embody your highest light, being willing to embody your true authenticity, letting go of the egoic need to compare your path with that of another, to compare your gifts with those of another ... and rather, consciously choosing to enter inward, to let go of the grasp on duality and comparison, to let go of the focus on the external.

And in this moment now, enter inward, tuning into the space inside of your center, the center of your chest, your heart, the center of your multidimensional being.

Let this energetic center, your heart portal, light up with divine presence, your authentic creative spark within illuminated with the golden plasma light of the divine, awakening your heart center to its highest authenticity.

Breathe into your heart and let this energetic center glow and grow more vibrant.

Expand and become more radiant.

Tune into the light of the divine you carry within you, the light of divine perfection, harmony, and vibrant well-being, the light of infinite possibility through your inherent unity and direct connection with the infinite, with everything that is in all existence.

Tune into this now by focusing on the area around your

heart center, the area around your body, the light, the divine presence, the infinite healing and frequency and radiant love that surrounds you in this moment.

Tune into this light around you as we, the Council of Light, assist this vibration in illuminating even more.

Know that as you keep your heart open and you shine with your authenticity, you join us in this act of elevating the vibration of the collective consciousness of humanity to consciously usher in a new paradigm of possibility for co-creation, for conscious advancement, ushering in a new wave of love and cooperation, advancement and creativity.

You call this forth by radiating out the coherent light of your heart, so that your heart light shines forth and into your surroundings.

You—through being an embodying love—radiate the coherent pattern empowered through your divine connection, empowered through the knowingness that through your open heart, you are linked with the infinite.

You are directly connected to the Divine.

You are able to access knowledge and guidance and healing and assistance in your manifestations and you are able to align with the vast possibilities available to you by opening your heart and letting it fill with this golden light—by letting this golden light expand around your body, around your mind, around your spirit.

In this golden light, begin to lift, so that you are like a sphere of golden energy.

A vast, huge pillar of light flows in from above and all around you, the pure presence of the divine, this column of light that you are now standing in, that is assisting you on every level, in letting go of the outdated and outworn, in letting go of perceived limitation and the feelings and emotions of being wronged or harmed.

In this moment now, tune into forgiveness, love, understanding, and neutrality—into all that has brought you to this very moment now where the light vibrantly glows within you and you are aware of the divine light brightly shining around.

You as an awakened divine being centered in your heart are able to now lift in this golden pillar of light, lifting up as if you are floating, lifting up in vibration as if you could fly, lifting up as if you're being carried up on wings of angels.

And as you lift, the archangels and seraphim, the masters of light reach down to connect with you in this moment now, to support you in this transformation where you are letting go of limitation and lack and you are re-accessing the infinite light and higher divine power of the divine being that you authentically are.

This high vibrational manifestation—these gifts of seeing, hearing, and knowing and the ability to consciously weave light and opportunity and possibility into creation—are now realigned. Your highest divine template is realigned in this moment.

It is as if the rungs of a ladder that were out of alignment suddenly click into sync, and your brainwaves and heart waves and your very vibration and energy signature in this moment come into coherence with the divine fabric of creation, with enlightened love, with the balanced masculine and feminine, bringing you in this moment into alignment with your highest authenticity and with the vast field of infinite possibility awaiting your instruction, awaiting your imprint, awaiting your direction.

For when you are resonant with your highest truth, your power within you rises to the surface and through your intention and through your knowing and through your planting the seeds, you can realign with the higher levels of your creativity … and not just for painting or coloring or writing.

The highest level of your creativity is to live as a creator being incarnate in physical form, here to write blessings into your reality, here to paint opportunities into your experience, here to color the pages of your book of life with vibrant beauty, joy, peace, and bliss.

And so, as your divine blueprint for your highest authenticity surrounds you, feel a sense of wholeness, of being supported and being loved ... for your dreams and aspirations, your creative nudges and curiosities, your joy is supported.

You are held up on the wings of angels as guided by the Divine.

You are supported in manifesting your destiny, living vibrantly and joyfully well, fulfilled and passionately inspired to accomplish your purpose through bringing your unique gifts and abilities to the surface and leveraging this unique light and power and strength and divine frequency in a way that realigns the collective consciousness, in a way that is in the highest interest of all.

You are an active participant in this transformation happening on your planet.

You are turning the page on the old and what has been and stepping into the new dawn of empowered, heart-centered, coherent consciousness, co-creating with love and joy and peace in consideration of All, of the One, of the Whole, of the Infinite that you are a part of.

With this being your North Star, there are of course waves to navigate and hurdles to jump. There is of course the old energy in many cases holding on, causing struggle and hardship that is quite simply not required.

But when you, in the moment, return to presence and consciously choose to realign your heart center with the light of love—regardless of what is happening in the external—you then, as an individual, consciously choose the paradigm of love and peace.

And when you broadcast this wavelength, it begins to

create in your life.

Your reality begins to transform, to bring this coherent love signature into the tangible, into the physical.

And as you continue to send out these coherent wavelengths of love, it becomes more effortless for those around you to come into this same sync, into this pattern, holding the template for the new paradigm of how life can be on Earth.

We invite you to let go of the overwhelm at how much needs to change to bring this reality to fruition. We encourage you to trust and simply play your part.

Live your authentic truth.

Come into sync and resonance with your highest light, for this creates a ripple.

And when all—and even when 70%—are in alignment with their highest light (and this does not even mean fully embodying it, but rather, simply being aware of and holding the intention to embody and call this forth), massive change and the doors of new possibility open to a new level, elevating the vibration of the collective consciousness and reuniting the consciousness of humanity with the infinite light of divine love.

And through this resonance, the highest divine qualities of the heart are able to spring forth, tangibly manifesting in a way that is in the highest interest of all, the highest fulfillment, love, joy, and cooperation.

In the interim, you're embodying love, you're shining your light, you're returning consciously to "All is well." Holding the field of love and light brings the blessings of this coherence into your own life.

And so, stay positively focused on the inspired, empowered future you as an individual are moving into, moving in the direction of your joy and fulfillment, your love, your bliss, your curiosity, knowing this too manifests throughout the level of All That Is.

And wherever great change is being called forth, so too is great support. Become aware in this moment of your team of light, your team of guides, your team in spirit who serve and love and assist you from beyond the veil.

Become aware of the angels and masters and star beings and loved ones and ancestors and guides who are lifting you up, encouraging you, and supporting you in every moment and in this moment now. And know that it is the love vibration, open heart, coherent waves that enable you to tune into the direct guidance and insight to receive direction and assistance.

Ask for support, ask for help, ask for guidance, ask for intervention, but then meet that guidance halfway.

Elevate your light.

Open your heart.

Take steps in the direction of your dreams and goals, for through this, you invite the support of spirit at a new level. For you are not here to be a third-party bystander; you are here to be an active participant, a divine being, an angelic creator in physical form.

We flow our blessings of light, awakened consciousness, and divine heart qualities this way, to empower you to lift and stand in the fullness of the light that you are, to step into sync and harmony into your highest potential.

This is the door opening for you now.

Your creative nudges, your inspiration—your act of lovingly parenting your mind and noticing when you are in doubt or fear, and consciously choosing to shift and return to love and peace and presence—is how you empower yourself to usher in the highest potentials for your life, beckoning you and inviting you into the new paradigm now.

You are supported, you are guided, you are loved, you are assisted … but this is your path.

Open your heart, tune into the immense light, power, and radiant love all around you, receiving the clarity of what is your next step. And then take it, trusting that the next will appear, ushering in your highest authenticity, your most vibrant service, your most radiant love as you stand in the fullness of the infinite divine being you authentically are.

When you shine your light and love, this indeed has a profound impact on all that is. And so, love and shine. And as you do, we offer our love and light to support and guide and assist you further.

Feel or imagine your feet planted on the surface of the earth and know that you are exactly where you are meant to be at this very point in time.

All that has happened has brought you right here and now, and this moment now is exactly when and where you access the new level of your light and authenticity, the new level of alignment with your higher self, the next level of embodiment of your divine being.

There is always a further step; there is always a next step ... but for right now, let yourself take a moment to simply open your heart and bask in the light.

Be uplifted, experiencing the magic and possibility, the divine perfection and harmony, the beautiful, radiant, incredible light and power of who you authentically are.

Notice how good it feels to be you, to be who you really are, refreshed, recharged, and realigned with your path of highest authenticity, knowing that your intuition, inspiration, joy, and love guide you further on this path.

Listen, trust, and act.

We are with you.

And so, it is…

21 EXPANDED DIVINE LIGHT

Take a moment to find a comfortable and relaxed position.

Breathe and become aware of an incredible supply of light and love that is all around you, nurturing you and uplifting you, supporting you and cleansing you, assisting you in lifting into a peaceful, tranquil, high vibrational state now in which you can shift your awareness within.

Focusing now on your heart center, the center of your multidimensional being, breathe light into this area to animate this center and to consciously expand your heart light around you. You may envision a brilliant orb or spiral of light above your head, representing your highest divine self and your direct link to the infinite, divine Creative Source, the pulse of all creation.

And from this golden spiral of light, imagine that energy is being channeled down into your heart center, replenishing your heart light, replenishing your inner light, and raising your life force energy from within.

As your heart light expands around you, surrounding your entire being, filling your entire room, calling in love vibration all around, become aware of your feet placed on the floor.

Then, from your heart center, envision your energy streaming downward, down through your legs, down through your feet, down through a root network grounding you to Gaia, Mother Earth, grounding you in the present moment. And with your energy, so too is your awareness now tuned into this root network below your feet.

Understand that these roots are the cumulative experiences of your lifetimes in the physical, of your interactions in this physical life, both positive and dense.

Become aware of the roots and any areas where there is density tied to memory or pain or challenge, and notice these vast stretching golden roots reaching down any areas of stagnant energy where the energy is vibrating slower, feeling denser, heavier, or darker.

Now, from the source light above you and from your open heart, send down the vibration of love, forgiveness, peace, and any additional positive quality of the divine which comes into your awareness. Send down these positive divine qualities into the earth and into your own root network, connecting you to the collective consciousness and to your multidimensional experiences on the planet across dimensions and across the lines of time.

Love, forgiveness, neutrality flow down to these areas of density.

Now, imagine around your entire being a great pillar of light, the pillar of light of your highest divine self, the direct divine presence of your highest authenticity, the divine pillar of light all around you.

In an upward pull from deep within the earth, from your personal root network, these lower vibrations and dense energies are pulled up, pulled up into this pillar of light and effortlessly released up into the Divine, returning to Source, returning to the light, releasing up, arcing out and returning to source.

Your feet and legs may begin to tingle with energy. They may feel heavy and then light as density across the lines of time, as past wounds and records within duality stored in the energetic root system are released.

And as this upward flow according to divine will unfolds, feel light and love and forgiveness around your entire being.

Let your heart expand to create a container of compassion and understanding and forgiveness, for all that has transpired to free you from the energetic weights of your past, the past emotional reactions, the past habitual responses, the past default modes of thinking or feeling tied to memory, tied to assumption, tied to this dense energy that from your root system, from your feet, and from your lower chakra energy centers is now released into the divine, into the light.

And now, from above, from this divine pulse of creation,

pure Source presence channels down along your spinal column.

It flows along this ascension pillar of light, down through the bottom of your feet, ushering in a fresh supply of pure Source presence, love, light, peace, tranquility into your root system, so that the roots connecting you to Gaia, connecting you to the physical, connecting you to the earth are translucent.

Golden, high vibrational, pure divine light—connecting you now to the higher dimensional crystalline grid of Gaia, the grid of the awakened earth, the higher dimensional earth and the golden light and divine possibility and higher dimensional opportunity—is available to you.

It is available to those who are tuned in and grounded and plugged into this higher dimensional earth experience.

The new earth is not another planet. It is this planet, yet you are tuning into the new earth experience now, birthing the blessings of the new earth from within the old.

And now, feel the golden light of the crystalline grid of the new earth that you are a part of, that you are connected to, rising up through the bottom of your feet, circulating crystalline energy up through your being, uniting you to the enlightened earth, the awakened earth, the crystalline grid of Gaia, Mother Earth, in this moment now.

This earth light flowing up meets the pure divine presence of your higher self in your heart center which is now further expanded, receiving the light of Gaia, the light of the Divine, the light of your highest authenticity.

Feel the container of your heart light expand out around you as you become more vast, as you become more embodied as a divine being in physical form. Let your heart light expand and let any density stored in your heart center dissolve into the light.

Return to Source and be transformed into love through your presence, through your forgiveness, through your intention now, to embody your highest possible potential, to embody your true divine nature, to live as the awakened divine angelic being in physical form, to embody all this that you authentically are.

And with this intention, your vibration is elevated further. Any lingering attachment or density or ties to duality in mind, body, emotion, spirit are transformed into divine presence, so that you in this moment now embody more of your true divine nature.

You may feel this as electric energy throughout your being—golden light shining within and all around you, returning your solar Christed divine nature and all the power and gifts and abilities of your divine physical being to you in this present.

And with your heart open, expanding around you, let yourself send love out, a wave of love out across the planet, across the galaxy, a wave of love transcending time and space, flowing forth into the infinite.

With this, you step into your power to serve through love and to make a difference through your simply being and embodying, being clear, being vibrant, transmuting negativity and past challenges into love.

And from this clear centered space, receive the knowing of what your next step is.

What is your next creative project as a divine creator being in the physical?

What is your next modality of being of service which you are able to do more effectively when you are clear, centered, and shining your full light of embodied love?

Once again, tune into the great pillar of light all around you, cleansing and elevating the energy along your spine, allowing your life force energy to flow upward and travel up from below your feet, up through your chakras, up through your heart, throat, third eye, crown, and into oneness and resonance with the divine pulse of light, with the infinite power of creation, of Source that you are a part of.

And focus once again on your heart center that receives an additional transmission of this direct Source presence, a love download direct from the Divine, to recalibrate you in this moment, vibrationally restoring your highest authenticity. And now—through your action, intention, service, one step at a time—you weave this, your authentic divine nature into physical being.

This is your role as a co-creator.

This is your role as a creation angel, a creation pillar of light, to become aware of your full vastness, to bask in it, to expand in it, to shine it forth and then to anchor this through intention and action into the physical.

Standing as a clear pillar of purity and divine authenticity, you, by default, serve to elevate the vibration of the collective consciousness, the earth and all. Standing as a pillar and then consciously co-creating, you fulfill your highest destiny, your highest purpose which you are now divinely supported in moving into alignment with now.

Do not let the vastness of what you have imagined this to be overwhelm you.

Let it continue to appear one moment at a time by choosing presence, by maintaining your clarity, by banishing fear and returning to love and anchoring the full light that you are through your being and through consistent, deliberate, inspired action.

You are guided and supported and loved as you continue on this path, transforming the world from within, transforming your life from within through embodiment and then through tangible action in the world around.

You have our love and blessings and support.

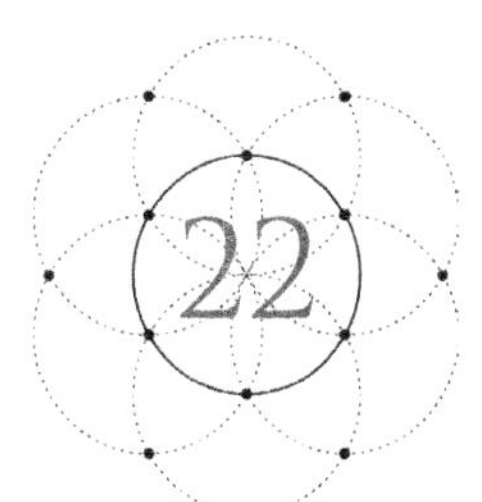

CRYSTALLINE BLESSINGS OF LIGHT

At this time in your present space, we greet you with love, with light, and with the encoded frequency of your divine blueprint, the energy of your vibrant health, authenticity, abundance, joy, and awakened light.

As this light streams in all around you from every direction—above, behind, below, beside, around, and from within—let yourself consciously relax your physical body, creating openings for the light to fill you. And relax your mind, allowing your awareness to enter in.

Breathe, relax, and let go as you now focus upon the light at the center of your being, the light of your open heart.

Tuning into the light of your heart and focusing in this energetic space, breathing light into your heart as you exhale, feel the light flowing throughout your entire body.

Breathe in the light and let the light flow into every cell.

Let it flow into your heart, which connects you to the great central sun, the source of light on the inner planes that broadcasts direct divine presence, awakened consciousness, crystalline harmonic resonance for you to now deeply attune to.

Through simply relaxing, you empower yourself to receive the light into your physical being, into every cell, allowing the light to push out and release at the cellular level, any distortions, negativity, incoherence, and fear.

Release into the light and allow the light of love, compassion, vitality, harmony, and peace to fill you, to fill every cell, raising the vibration of every cell of your being. This may feel like lifting, expanding, floating.

And as you begin to lift and float in this light, become aware of your feet filled with light. Become aware of the core of light along your spinal column.

With your awareness, focus on this core of light.

Draw light into your physical being, into your physical core, which will begin raising your vibration physically, tangibly filling your physical being with light, preparing your physical vessel to embody the higher levels of your soul light consciousness and awareness.

As you do so, recognize that you are indeed, a spiritual being in physical form. But you are physical for a good reason; your soul journey includes being physical, really being here in the present, on the earth, in your body, where you are able to receive and anchor, embody and shine with a new level of radiance.

An unprecedented level of light flows through your inner being, filling your heart, filling your spinal column, filling your ascension pillar of light.

The light from your heart flows up, up from your heart, into your throat, your mind's eye, your crown, your soul star chakra above your head. The pillar of light flows up into the infinite spiritual realms and flows down from your heart, grounding you to the earth, grounding you to the crystalline core of earth, connecting you to All That Is.

Become aware of the cycle of light flowing up from the earth, up along your ascension column, up into your pineal gland, unlocking your clairvoyance, continuing up into direct presence with the Divine, Source, All That Is.

And envision this incredible light flowing down, pouring back down around you in the toroidal flow of energy and light and flowing directly down from Source—in through your crown, down along your spinal column, down through the bottom of your feet, to the core of the earth and arcing back up in reverse.

Your Taurus light body is now accelerating in vibration and receiving a divine realignment and attunement to simplify this energetic opening.

You may simply envision the energy spiraling around you in a counterclockwise motion as your entire energy field, aura, and light body are cleansed and purified and opened to their highest potential.

This energy is energetically paving the way for you as a physical being to embody and shine with more of your light and radiance.

And so, as you experience this vortex counterclockwise flow of energy, let yourself let go and enter in, into your heart, into your physical body, into the space of your inner being, aware of the light spiraling around you, aware of the light shining within you.

Dive into that inner light.

Dive into the inner light to experience it both within and around, to experience now through your heart center, your direct link with the infinite supply of light on the inner realms.

Receive—through this link, through this golden ray of crystalline consciousness—the cleansing energy, the rejuvenating energy, the activating, initiating and uplifting energy, the golden Christ consciousness energy of your true divine blueprint and highest enlightened nature.

Receive the light into your heart. Receive the light that supercharges the column of light along your spine, so that your heart is receiving its own Taurus energy field accelerating in vibration and shining forth beyond you.

The light of love, the light of hope, the light of awakening, fills your surroundings with light, fills your home, your country, the earth, the galaxy, with light from the inner planes which is also manifest externally through your radiance, through your awakened creativity, through your inspiration, through your joy and vitality.

The light from your heart expands to fill your energy,

to fill your aura, shining through any grayish haze and illuminating the energy of your body, mind, and spirit with white, golden crystalline light.

Feel this divine recalibration. The haze or fog dissolves into the golden light, allowing more of this inner light and more of the external light to fill you, to fill your hands and your feet with golden tingling light.

Any sensation you may experience is a mere validation of this flow of light and energy unlocking, unlocking the doors, so that your divinely awakened potential can spring forth, energetically, physically, tangibly aligning you with the highest divine possibilities, the highest divine blueprint, the highest divine timeline for you to embody your full light.

Become aware of every cell shining with light.

Become aware of the space around you and your ability to now claim this space.

And from your open heart, which is directly linked to the infinite source of light through simple awareness, you are able to fill your heart with light, fill your body with light, fill your aura with light, fill your space with light.

We wish for you to know this simple process of shining your light is some of the most powerful foundational work for you in creating physical tangible change in your experience.

Paving the pathway of light aligns opportunity,

impossibility, creative inspiration, and divine guidance for how to then create with this light through your action, to step into the new paradigm, the new paradigm that is emerging from within the old.

As you witness institutions and structures and past constructs fading, crumbling, perhaps even dramatically falling away, remember that out of the old, the new is emerging.

And when you stay connected to your inner source of light and harmony and bliss, when you stay centered in the present moment, your direct link to the Divine, to the infinite light and power realized, there is always opportunity, always a way.

In this time in which you live of the new earth emerging from within the old, be attuned to your inspirations and creative ideas and visions for how you may be of service and contribute value in a way that you love and enjoy, in a way that inspires and excites you and serves in alignment with the highest interest of all.

This is awakened high vibrational living—living in the new paradigm, living as an awakened, embodied divine being in physical form, returning to awareness, centering and being present here and now.

And yes, we will continue to work with you to lift, to fill yourself with light, to expand your awareness and to experience beyond the physical in magical, joyful ways.

But recognize this beyond the physical—while an essential piece of the puzzle—is all in an effort for you to anchor this higher dimensional awareness into your physical body, into your life, into your heart, into your every cell, as an embodiment of your light and divine blueprint and co-creation with the infinite light of the divine in the physical.

At this time, the full presence of your highest divine self steps forward for you to experience, for you to embody, for you to shine as and claim this true divine nature as yours.

Through this merge of mind, body, spirit, light, you are able to glimpse your highest service, how you may joyfully and lovingly make a difference in a multifaceted way through simply shining, loving, living vibrantly well, way-showing.

You find this highest service through your specific guided action.

You find it through intention and inspiration and through both areas—physical and nonphysical, action and inaction—infusing all you do through your open heart, through the inner light of love, allowing light to flow throughout your entire experience, harmonizing your way ahead and aligning you with the new possibility you have already expanded into.

You are now in a process of realizing the possibilities of this new expanded state of being, realizing the possibilities within this new paradigm, vibrantly thriving within the old, choosing to detach from the old, to let go of the past, to be fully present here and now.

Your heart is open, your ascension column filled with light, your inspiration clear, your gifts and awareness awakened, your love vibration flowing through your entire being, harmonizing, balancing, even healing and rippling this coherent love, the blessings of the light far beyond, through your energy, through the coherent crystalline waves you are sending out.

Vote for peace, for harmony, for balance, for vitality, for love.

Let the light of your heart shine forth to positively uplift, bless, inspire every aspect of your experience and—extending out far beyond that—to bless, uplift, harmonize and realign the collective consciousness with the same inner source of infinite divine light that you are always able to access through your open heart, flowing it forth, rippling it out, shining it brightly, to joyfully uplift, inspire, and abundantly thrive and to serve with love in the highest interest of all.

The potentials before you are bright.

The opportunities are vast.

And we are honored to guide and love and support you as you continue upon this path of truly embodying all that you are, not only in meditation, not only in prayer or contemplation, but through action, through being, through doing, through experiencing, through embodying the fullness of the inner divine being that you are, both inwardly and externally in the highest interest of all.

Keep shining, keep your heart open, and love will continue to guide you. And return in the present to this experience of your heart, open, directly linked to the great central sun, to All That Is, to the light.

Receive and flow forth to benefit all.

We love you and we bless you.

Take a moment to send your heart this same love and blessing. Send your body love and blessings. Send the collective consciousness your love and blessings, knowing the power of love, the power of blessing can truly positively change, inspire, awaken, heal, resolve with blessing for all.

Receive the blessing and flow it forth.

Open to a new level. Shine with a new light. Step into a new day.

Live in the new, in the now, in love.

And so, it is…

23 YOUR HIGHEST DIVINE LIGHT BEING

Greetings from the Council of Light—we, who have ascended to fully embody our highest divine light being, who connect with you in this moment now, outside of time and space, with love and frequency and healing light and energy to support you in the same, in connecting with, experiencing, and embodying your highest divine light being.

And to begin, we invite you to let go.

Let go of the worries of the day or week or year.

Let go of whatever is left on your schedule or to-do list.

Let go just for now of your focus upon the external world around you and enter inward, entering into your heart.

As you now breathe in, envision light flowing into your heart center, activating the sacred portal and access point to the higher dimensions of experience.

And as you exhale, let this light expand.

And now, with your inward intention, let yourself intend to connect with the full light and presence of your highest divine light, the highest light of your inner divine being.

Stay focused upon your heart center as the presence of your highest divine being streams in all around you. Feel the light of this presence above, below, all around and within.

As you begin to embody your highest divine being in this moment here and now, let yourself release constructs of your ego mind, any energies or lower entities tied to patterns of thought or beliefs or attachments or limitations that no longer serve.

And through your open heart—expanding in awareness to more fully experience and embody your divine beingness—now expand and lift, entering deeper into your heart center and lifting now on the wings of love, on the wings of angels into a higher dimensional experience of divine light that transcends the language spoken, that transcends the concepts of your mind, for true Divine Source connection is beyond language, time, and mind.

Expand to experience this now, your awareness expanding to fill your room with the light of your inner divine being. Become aware of the light all around you, glittering and sparkling with divine crystalline harmony.

Expand to let this light fill your home, your city, state, and the entire globe glowing with the divine crystalline plasma light.

And now, become aware of the entire Milky Way galaxy as your heart center expands for you to have an experience of oneness with this galactic level of consciousness with the highest divine light of the entire galaxy.

Become aware of your oneness with this and with all that is.

And now, allow this awareness to focus to the very center of the galaxy where you tune in now to pure crystalline plasma divine light which streams down in a river of divine perfection, a waterfall of coherent love towards your physical body in this present moment, at this very time.

Allow this crystalline divine plasma light from the galactic level of consciousness to cleanse your being, to flush out any lower vibratory frequencies, to flow into any spaces of stuck or stagnant energy, to completely revitalize and re-harmonize your mind, body, spirit, light with the crystalline codes of awakening and divine crystalline cosmic light.

Let this light fill your body, flowing along your central ascension column, flowing in through the top of your head and down along this ascension column, out through the bottom of your feet, anchoring the crystalline divine light to the earth.

Feel your oneness and connection to the earth and to All That Is as this cosmic flow of light continues, you at the center of it, being completely illuminated, cleansed, uplifted, recharged, and activated, so that you may more fully embody your highest divine light, accessing all your gifts and awareness and wisdom across the lines of time.

And at any time, when you notice a thought, the ego mind chiming in, know that you are able to minimize this ego as you would a window on your computer, thinking your ego and asking it to simply focus upon the light and to support you in more fully receiving the crystalline downloads available to you now.

As you, in the physical, receive these downloads of light, let yourself once again return to the awareness of the galactic level of consciousness, tuning into the entire Milky Way galaxy and to the highest divine light of this galactic consciousness.

Expand now further to experience your direct connection with the infinite transcendent one true God, Source, infinite, prime creative light, minimizing the thoughts as they appear and expanding more fully into the transcendent experience of divine love, witnessing the intricate, detailed and vast connections with All That Is, with everything in creation and everything that has yet to be created.

Expand into this level of Source God consciousness.

You may experience this as the sensation of crystalline plasma light sparkling within every cell of your physical being; feelings of lifting, flying, or floating; or nothing at all.

As you repeat this session, your experience will be enriched as you relax and let go of the need to record or understand or analyze, judge or even remember, knowing that these are functions of the ego which can be minimized and asked to simply focus upon the transcendent light, so that you may more fully expand to bask in and simply experience all that you are.

And now, the highest and most expensive level of this God consciousness which you are able to embody and carry in the present returns with you to your physical body in this present point in time, merging with mind, body, and spirit.

Know that as you return awareness now to your physical body, you do so with the overlay of your highest divine blueprint, which is a divine hologram of your highest divine expression that works now to bring back into coherence any area of your being that has fallen out of sync.

You do not need to understand where or how or in what form this is working. Just trust that a realignment and recalibration is unfolding.

Tune into the light of your heart, knowing that through your sacred heart center, you have—in this and every moment—access to your inner divine being who retains the full and complete awareness of transcendental God, Source consciousness, galactic consciousness, crystalline consciousness, earth consciousness, and the divine blueprint of perfection for your physical template and vibrant physical well-being.

We remind you now of this awareness, for you are at a powerful point of new beginning, where you are invited to step into a new level of sovereignty, living in the physical as your highest divine being.

In each present moment is your opportunity to more fully practice and embody this highest light, through presence, awareness, and love.

We are here to support you. The angelic realm is here to support you and your highest divine light being is here to support you in aligning your physical with the highest potential timeline, with the primary ascension timeline for you to progress along now, embodying, shining as, thriving in the physical, in oneness with your highest divine being.

We are here to support you at any time. You are loved.

As you return now to the physical, to your body, know that you have experienced a profound reset.

Remember, you have the ability to minimize the ego mind, lovingly asking the ego to focus upon the light, so that you can return your perspective to that of your highest divine being.

The ego has its role to remember dates and locations and to respond to aspects of the physical, but let this be the role of the ego and let the bigger picture be fulfilled by your higher divine mind and embodiment of your highest light.

Feel your heart light refreshed and revitalized.

Feel the light—the crystalline level of consciousness—

glittering throughout your entire body and being.

Consciously tune into this golden sparkling energy smiling within you.

Be sure to smile back and ... through this ... send out waves of blessing, light, and crystalline coherence through your reality.

Let this action begin to align the blessings of your primary ascension timeline, your true soul purpose, your true divine nature, your highest soul mission in this life, on this timeline, in this body, through this, your experience now.

We love you.

We bless you.

We honor the sovereign divine light being you are now.

Thank you, thank you, thank you…

24 COSMIC CONNECTION

At this time, let yourself relax, get comfortable, and shift your awareness within as the quality of energy around you is uplifted, as pure source light and crystalline divine presence stream in on the 12 rays from every direction, entering into this exact moment now where we meet outside of time and space, to lift, to expand, to restore and illuminate your highest divine presence, ready to be embodied through your physical being.

Understand that any tension or frustration you have been experiencing is a direct result—or some may call a symptom—of the higher levels of light, the codes of crystalline consciousness and the divine codes of your highest authenticity that are streaming into your present reality like upgrades to a computer program.

These codes of authenticity seek to upgrade every aspect of your life by expanding your conscious perspective, so that you may embody a more fully realized blueprint of your highest divine authenticity.

The codes anchor in through your heart center, through your physical body, into each and every cell. The codes of your highest authenticity download into your mental being, into your emotional being, into your aura, into your personal energetic signature.

Understand that through this, no area of your personality is meant to stay as it has been. Who you have been is a vastly limited snapshot and who you are is now expanding, uplifting, opening for you to have an experience of your true divine nature—transcending ego, personality, and identity to tune into the vastness, the oneness of Divine Source presence.

At this time, let your awareness focus upon your heart center, becoming aware of the tempo of your physical heartbeat.

And with each beat of your heart, like the beating of a drum, your heart light expands around you and the heartbeat brings up to the surface anything that has been blocking your expansion such as belief or past pain, feeling unworthy, and low self-esteem.

Any of that old energy—which is stagnant and lower vibrationally—is dislodged and dispersed and released into the light of pure divine presence. And as you release, your vibration effortlessly expands, for your container holds more space.

Tune into the space within you, along your core and your spinal column, now filling with the light of the 12 rays. The colors of divine creation in both the visible and non-visible spectrum fill your core with crystalline light.

Let this core of light expand around you, preparing you—mind, body, and spirit—to embody your highest divine presence now. Expand out through your heart to embody your divine being.

Your every cell, every body system, raises its light quotient as your energy expands for your highest authenticity, your true divine beingness, to be made known to you, to shine through you in this moment now.

Let your heart light continue to increase in radiance and expand around you, expanding to fill your room, expanding to the earth level consciousness, the light of your heart shining like an inner sun.

Become aware of your direct link through your heart center, to the great central sun.

You may imagine this as if you're standing upon the earth, basking in the most beautiful sunlight. It streams in not from one physical source and location, but from every direction, from below, behind, and all around ... activating your light body, activating your inner solar Christ light.

Become aware of the many angels and guides who are with you, supporting you now in lifting, expanding, and letting go of the layers of illusion, letting go of the frustrations and fears, simultaneously letting go, opening, lifting, and entering inward, lowering downward, so that you rise up.

Your highest divine being meets you there, lifting you even further.

Expand and lift on the pure coherent light waves that you are sending out and that are all around you. Lift on the wings of the angels who support you now as you are lifting to link with the higher dimensional light of the crystalline grid.

Become aware of the crystalline grid and your oneness therein. Receive the ascension downloads, the codes of awakening, the codes of your highest authenticity available to you now.

Authenticity as a crystalline physical being rises up through your open heart to meet your highest divine light being. Expand in presence to embody your highest divine being at the level of the crystalline grid where you effortlessly receive and send forth love, blessing, and the energies of awakening to benefit your life and to ripple out far beyond you through your personal energetic signature to benefit all.

Receive and give.

Refresh and flow forth.

At this level, your masculine and feminine energies are united as one. Envision your heart opening to a new dimension like a lotus flower opening up within you, opening towards the light of the great central sun, opening up, expanding into your galactic level of awareness and consciousness.

Imagine you're lying on your back, floating in a pool of

starlight, floating atop the Milky Way galaxy, the space and void gently holding you, the light of the stars all around you, illuminating you, recalibrating and balancing you, restoring your direct connection with this galactic level of consciousness.

And now, within the galaxy, you are able to find the very center, the galactic core.

As you enter into it, you expand further, becoming aware of the vast web of connections connecting everything, letting go of your identity, letting go of all that has been, relaxing and expanding into the nothingness, into everything and nothing, into the transcendental experience of God consciousness that is not separate from you, that you are.

Expand into the infinite light which now begins to flow down.

The light of pure Divine Source, the galactic level of consciousness, the light of the crystalline grid, the light of the awakened earth stream downward, stream inward, flow in all around you in this present moment, completely cleansing your being like a divine cosmic flash, flushing out from your physical body all that no longer serves.

It flushes out from your emotional being all that is ready to let go, clearing out and releasing from mind, body, spirit all that is inharmonious, incongruent, and out of alignment.

Simultaneously, the light is filling and uplifting your being, expanding your perspective, so that you now become aware of the presence of your highest divine being at an entirely new level, one which transcends your individuality.

Your highest divine presence is in unity with all.

And with this oneness as a new foundation, you are now able to anchor the highest possibilities, the highest level of authenticity for your individuality.

You are becoming aware now—through specifics or through a simple subtle feeling—of all that is possible for you to be, do, have, and experience in your life as your highest divine self aligns you with this now.

And now, imagine that you are calling back, calling back to the layer and level of your highest divine self any incongruent energy you have sent out, any inharmonious creations, thought patterns, past actions, ideas, or possibilities that you have initiated, but that are out of alignment with your highest joy and love and authenticity and truth.

Call back the distortions, limitations, fears, insecurities—not to the level of your physical being, but to the level of your highest divine being who effortlessly receives all that is not love, all that is not truth, all that does not serve.

Let your highest divine being receive these through the calling back of any fragmented or distorted timelines you have set into motion through fear or worry or default programming.

These return now to the level of your highest divine self to be healed, harmonized, dissolved, and returned to infinite Source light, as you call back that which at the level of your truth and authenticity and the highest level of love, is not what you really want to create.

Your highest divine self releases these.

And now, just focus on your heart as this process takes a few moments.

You may remember certain events where you have said things you did not mean or want, or took action that was not authentically you and true.

You may remember aspects of your past self as these things are called back from the vibrational field of creation to be healed, realigned, dissolved, or released.

And your heart glows brighter.

Become aware of the orb of golden light within your heart, the divine light and presence flowing along your core.

Become aware of the multi-levels, multiple dimensions of your true self, the galactic level of your consciousness blissfully floating among the stars, your connection to everything through the infinite web of creation. Guided by your highest divine self, you now send out through this web of creation the pure vibration of love.

Each beat of your heart sends out a pulse of coherent energy, aligning in your outer world the love and peace and truth of your inner being.

You now have an opportunity to focus on what it is you really want. Perhaps this is on a global scale, a vision or feeling of heaven on Earth. Perhaps this is a physical level of true abundance, vibrant well-being, blissful joy, and love.

Focus upon the feeling of what you really want.

See the mental picture of what this looks like, feels like, sounds like, tastes like.

And now, imagine that this beautiful and inspiring vision and feeling is now compressed down into a golden seed of light that you are able to plant inside of your heart center, which brings a level of healing and excitement and love to your heart and which is perfectly nurtured and tended by your love and by your embodying your highest light and authenticity.

You may begin to now see this seed begin to bud and grow, transforming into a plant and then into a flower. Its petals open and reach towards the light, representing the manifestation of your highest intention and your vision into being in alignment with your true divine nature, with your highest authenticity, with your radiant inner divine bliss and love.

Feel the light of your heart flowing upward along your

ascension column of light, into your throat, your mind and your crown, circling all around you, filling out your light body, revitalizing your aura and supporting your physical form.

And feel your heart light flowing downward, down along your ascension column, along your legs and out your feet, into the earth, all the way to the core, grounding you to the core of Gaia, Mother Earth, who graciously receives any lingering fears or frustrations or tensions in your physical body, any pain.

Allow this to drain out through your ascension column, through your grounding column, to the core of Gaia, Mother Earth who you are one with and who receives and releases this at her level of highest divine being.

Tune into your gratitude for the earth, gratitude for all that has happened on your path, and gratitude for the beauty and opportunity and inspiring light of your inner vision of what is truly possible moving into the new, into the new earth.

Focus on your highest authenticity, your divine light and inspiration, your inner guidance, your vibrant vitality and love available to you in every moment through your open heart and through remembering your greater level of love and harmony and oneness with the earth, humanity, the crystalline grid, the angelic and celestial realms, galactic consciousness, the great central sun and pure Divine Source light and presence.

Expand to know and experience your true authenticity and all that you truly are.

Return now awareness to your physical heart … each heartbeat, each breath, a reminder of your expanded divine self and your ability—through presence, through love, through coherence, through awareness—to create love within you, around you, and with every heartbeat rippling out beyond you to benefit, serve and assist, according to divine will, in the highest interest of all.

We love you and we bless you.

And so, it is…

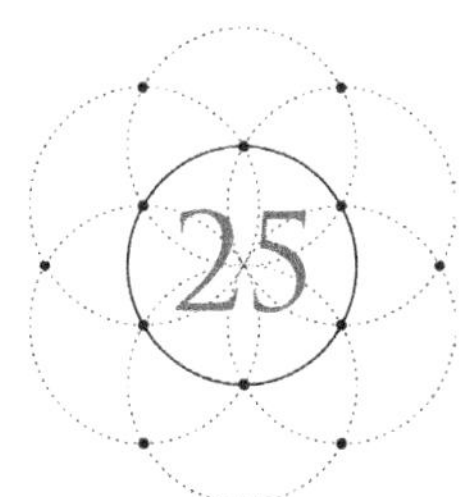

CREATING AS A DIVINE BEING

Breathe and begin to focus your awareness inward. Relax and know that we, the Council of Light, are here, greeting you in this present moment with an infinite supply of love, paving the way for the light codes and frequencies to enter into your being, to enter into the present moment, to support you in fully activating and experiencing and connecting with the part of you that knows how to embody your highest divine self.

And now—by focusing inward on your heart center in your own unique way of opening, expanding, lifting, and dropping in—let yourself embody the highest light of your inner divine being.

Feel the presence of your divine self within and far around your physical form, allowing yourself permission to relax, to let go of any attachment to outcome or sensation, to let go of the part of you that wants to record and contemplate the experience of embodiment.

As you let go, as you expand into the infinite light around you—just being, opening, allowing and lifting—loving yourself in this moment for simply showing up, loving what is and loving the possibilities before you, remember that love is what paves the pathway for your highest light to flow in, to rise up.

And so, imagine now that you're breathing love into every cell, in through your lungs and also indirectly to every cell, so that your toes are breathing in love, which allows the light to flow in.

Your ankles, calves and legs are breathing in the love vibration, cultivating a new inner level of light within your physical being.

Breathe love into your knees, allowing the light to flow in, breaking up any resistance or fear. Breathe the love into your thighs and your hips, letting go of any attachment to drama or pain, allowing a new level of light to flow in.

Breathe the love into your abdomen that fills with light. Breathe love into your entire back, your chest, your arms, your wrists. Breathe love into your jaw, your neck, your ears and face, your brain and mind.

Breathe love into your entire physical body, allowing a new level of your divine light being.

Love paves the pathway for your deeper and more complete embodiment of light, of the divine light being you are.

And from here, your creation filled with light, you begin flowing light forth and grounding and anchoring light through your creativity, through your expression, through your writing, through your play and enjoyment, through your service.

When you allow the light to flow in and out, to flow in and through your actions, the light expands further.

Know that this opportunity is opening for you to create with and to express your love and light, which allows this vibration to expand, which allows for a more complete embodiment in every moment.

At this time, imagine that you're reaching up, that you're reaching, stretching upward to connect with an even higher divine part of yourself with your absolute highest divinity, your highest divine light potential, inspiration, and presence.

Reach way up into the light.

You may feel a sensation as if you're riding upward on an elevator or floating up in a balloon or lifting upward on a cloud.

Lift up into the light.

And now, with your energetic hands, imagine you're running your hands through the energy that represents your divine presence, your highest light. Run your fingers through it and notice the quality of energy of this brilliant light and love.

And now, listen with your inner ears for your divine soul tone—the tone of creation representing your highest embodiment of your divine individuality, your highest authentic truth.

Listen and feel for your divine soul tone.

And now, with your inner eyes, look for and see and receive a visual of the quality of your divinity. Picture the color and the texture of your light.

To support you, this golden plasma crystalline light flows into your mind's eye. It flows into the area of your pineal gland, stimulating, activating, and opening this psychic sense to a new level, so you can see who you really are as a divine being.

And now, with your inner sense of knowing, experience and know the highest level of your divine truth. Tuning into your heart center, as you glow with golden crystalline light, allow a higher level of your divine presence to embody a balance between lifting up and entering in, going deeper and expanding wider, allowing and being and shining as the awakened divine being in the physical you are.

And now, from your heart, send forth the love vibration of love, peace, and blessing to all awakened hearts making up the human heart grid.

Send love, blessings of peace, of ease, of kindness and compassion.

Send your blessings of love out to all who make up the human heart grid.

And now, allow yourself to receive in return the blessings of love, kindness, compassion, healing, joy, ease, and well-being from the awakened human heart grid. Send and receive this blessing of love that opens the flow for a new level of light to infuse and elevate the entire heart grid, activating each sacred heart with a new lightness.

A new chamber opens for divine expression and creation in a joyful, loving and rewarding way, elevating the light of the human heart grid.

As a result, the light of the entire planet and all of humanity rises to the next level. We invite you to now send your forgiveness to humanity, to send your forgiveness, love, and blessing of peace, ease, harmony, and compassion.

Reconnect with your divine being, the part of you that is able to observe All That Is with love, with divine neutrality—the part of you that is able to freely forgive and send your love and blessings to all beings.

This love creates an opening for a powerful healing through forgiveness and release for humanity as a whole and for the collective consciousness to come into resonance with the divine soul song of Gaia, of the divine blueprint for the awakened earth, for the earth to ascend into a new level of light and for humanity to support this ascension through consciously choosing—together as one—the vibration of love.

Return to the divine part of you that believes this to be possible. Return to the divine part of you, allowing a new level of your light to shine forth from you in this present moment.

And now, in this moment, embodying your divine self and light, send your love and blessing to all corners and stretches of your life to pave the pathway opening up before you with love, allowing a new level of light to shine through, to open the highest potentials, to align your highest divine timeline, to live in harmony with your soul tone, to live embodied as a light being in the physical, to live in true mastery of love.

Anchoring this light into the physical by sending your love and blessing and healing and kindness to the earth, now envision your light flowing down in a crystalline column of light all the way to the core of Gaia, Mother Earth, already embodying her highest ascended state.

Experience this crystalline light at the core of Gaia.

Experience your oneness with it.

Experience the light accelerating and opening to a new level, the Christ light at the core of the earth resonating in perfect harmony with your inner divine Christ light, triggering forth a wave of peace, grace, and ease, of love and of blessing for all beings.

You may now wish to move your hands, sway your body, circle your wrists and ankles and wiggle your toes as you feel the new level of light shining within you, as you feel the new level of your divinity shining beyond you, anchored into the present, into you.

You are this light. Create with it and it will continue to elevate.

Shine forth and glow.

We love you, we bless you, we are you, fully ascended and one with Divine.

Thank you.

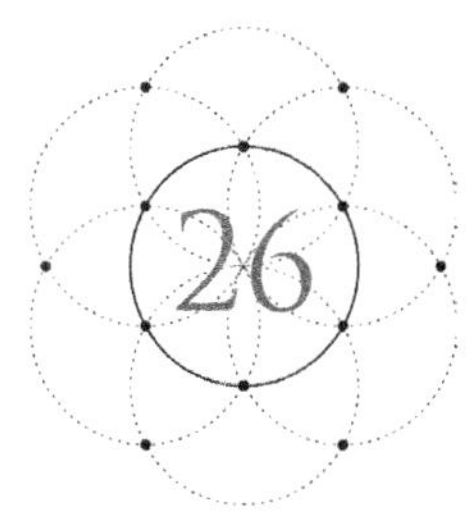

INCREASING YOUR RADIANCE

Greetings from the Council of Light.

We, in this moment, greet you with love and divine presence, inviting you to shift your awareness within, to open and expand your heart center, becoming aware of a pillar of light at the center of your being.

Now, shift your awareness in whatever way feels natural for you now, to embody a greater level of the light, of your inner divine being.

Silently feel yourself sending you a blessing of love.

You may think, *I love you,* or just open your heart and let the love vibration flow, creating an opening for a higher level of your light embodiment, a higher level of your divine presence to enter in, to be experienced, to shine through you and all you do.

Let your awareness now expand outward into the space around you, filled with the same divine quality, filled with light and love. And become aware of each of the members of the Council of Light, the ascended masters who surround you now.

We each stand in embodiment of the divine quality that will most serve you in integrating your embodiment at a new level. And these qualities are transmitted your way through this sharing of ascension codes.

Know that what you experience and what you are exposed to, you have the potential to integrate and to become.

And so, in this moment now, we broadcast and share with you, for you to experience and for you to integrate—if you are willing—pure divine qualities of the highest divine light.

Let yourself expand in this love, joy, peace, bliss, presence, willingness, openness, purity, determination, persistence, groundedness. Receive the divine qualities of compassion, elation, serenity, focus, presence, abundance, and whatever additional qualities are meant for you specifically in this moment now.

They are woven into this present point in time, infusing the air and the quality of energy around you, filling the space with an example, an experience of embodying the highest potentials and qualities of your inner divine light.

They are anchored and manifest through your physical form, through knowing all that you are, through feeling the vastness and elevated qualities of your light, through seeing your inner brilliance, knowing your inner divinity, embodying this higher level of the divine multidimensional being you are.

Turning up the level of your vibration now, let your heart open and expand into this experience as the love and light vibration circulate through every cell, through your entire multidimensional being.

Now, through your open heart, you are able to expand, to embody and experience all that you are—your highest potentials, the highest level of light which you as an individual can expand to experience and embody now.

Let yourself expand beyond your physical body, beyond the earth level consciousness, beyond crystalline consciousness, beyond the angelic level of consciousness, beyond the galactic consciousness, beyond the multiverse level of consciousness.

Expand and lift to journey through your conscious awareness into what is unknown, into greater vastness, greater light, and higher frequency than you personally have yet experienced.

Lift higher, filling with more light, coming into a deeper coherence with divine love and expanding in consciousness to experience Divine, Source, God consciousness now, beyond mind, beyond body, beyond your individual spirit, experiencing the vast connections of all—physical and nonphysical, spiritual and infinite.

And in this vastness of space and light, become aware of your highest divine expression at an individualized level, so that you are aware of the highest divine part of you.

Tune into this part of you that observes with non-judgment, loves with nonattachment, serves without a need for reciprocation.

We draw your awareness now to your physical body which is receiving a crystalline recalibration and an upgrade for you to more fully embody your highest divine light, for you to be able to access this divine connection, to feel it through your heart center, to speak and receive the messages of your highest divine truth through your throat, to see and understand through your third eye and to truly know at the level of your crown who you really are.

Vast potentials unfold as a result of you fully embodying your divine light while you are here in your physical vessel now illuminated with brilliant light.

The level of light of every cell is turned up in vibration as the space between yourselves is cleansed and elevated with pure golden crystalline light, and your body vehicle is attuned to your highest divine template for pure expression.

At this point, you may become aware of any areas of your body receiving further recalibration as golden, diamond, and rainbow light where it will most serve.

This light streams into areas of tension, areas of energetic blockage, areas simply in need of love, love which opens the energetic flow for the light to stream in and to flow through you.

Let yourself expand to embody now a higher level of your true light and your authentic expression, so that you are like a lighthouse, guiding others by simply being the light you are, shining light forth, staying in a state of love, being peaceful, present, aware, embodying the divine qualities and integrating them into your life.

This knowing you are divine, this knowing you are one with all, this knowing you are connected to the infinite and vast field of potential is not only a spiritual and meditative journey and experience.

Rather, you allow this "knowing" to flow forth into all areas of what you do, so that you might create in the world around you with love and light, to share and to give of your gifts and creativity.

And know that yes, indeed, when you flow forth your gifts, when you serve, when you shine your light, when you anchor the infinite potentials into the physical through your inspired ideas and action, your creation in physical form allows your light to grow even further.

So, here and now, you are invited to embody the highest level of vibration your physical template can hold.

But know that as you anchor this light—as you continue to practice this and other sessions, as you continue to experience meditative journeys and expand to the galactic level of consciousness, to divine consciousness, to embody all that you are at the individual level (and indeed, far beyond this, at the collective and unity consciousness level)—your physical template too expands and you progress.

You are thus able to reach what is higher than your current highest level of light. And so, simply experiencing the light opens you to more.

But then when you anchor this by being of service in a way you love and enjoy, by acting in the highest interest of all, you are progressing on the path of your soul purpose.

Through this, so too does your light quotient expand. Indeed, you are at a point of bringing new levels of your divinity into your conscious awareness and flowing them through all that you do.

There is support for you on this path and what may be considered the external, but which you of course are a part of.

We encourage you to use your discernment to uncover the meaning of the signs and symbols and dreams and guidance you receive, to take what serves, to let all that you receive on the inner and outer planes be the catalyst for your further growth ... both opportunity and challenge, both roadblock and open pathway.

Let all of creation, all of existence, usher you further into your highest embodiment of your divine light, your present work, hobbies, relationships. These all hold keys and opportunities.

You, in every present moment, have the potential to stay

centered in this higher dimensional awareness through which it is completely natural for you to respond with love.

If you fall short, let that be the opportunity to bounce back in return.

If you feel challenged, let that be your opportunity to return to presence.

This is a new beginning for you. And so, let yourself let go of what has been, to free yourself from the past, from trauma, knowing that it's okay if these things are still rising to the surface within you.

But you are supported now in letting them go. And with each release of the lower levels, so too are you able to expand to a new light.

Through release, through service, through anchoring your light, through creative action, through receiving inspiration and taking action to move you along the path of accomplishing your highest life purpose, your expansion into your highest embodiment takes shape and form.

Continue to return to the open heart, the sacred access point to the highest levels of divine light reaching downward, grounding you to the earth, reaching upward, anchoring you to the heavens, opening up and expanding around you, your ascension column glowing, a crystalline golden pillar of light at your core glowing with light from within, attracting light from around, increasing your radiance and anchoring the highest divine qualities of your highest authentic truth into the present, upon the earth, into the physical, through your life.

May you know, see, feel, understand, and receive the blessings available to you—embodying, shining, loving, being, creating as an awakened divine being thriving on the earth in your vibrant, healthy, happy, crystalline physical form.

As we step away, we flow a final surge, the divine qualities to most support you, to bless you right here and now.

We love you, we bless you.

And so, it is…

27 CREATING WITH YOUR HIGHEST LIGHT

Greetings from the Council of Light—

Indeed, it is through the embodiment of your highest divine expression within the physical that the true expansiveness of infinite possibility is accessible by you through embodiment.

You are able to create specific blessings and positive outcomes in your experience, both in alignment with your clear intention and in an expanded way that's even better than you can imagine from your present vantage point and perspective.

And so, let us begin.

As you focus your awareness within, as divine light and the energy of blessing stream in on every ray of divine light, elevating you in the present moment and raising the vibrational quality of energy of your surroundings, let yourself relax, breathe, and let go.

Imagine vast space and light all around you, gently holding you in this present point in time.

And now, shift your awareness within, focusing on the

inner space behind your eyes, behind your throat, behind your heart, opening and entering inward, opening your heart. And now, with your inner intention, invite your highest divine self to fully unite with you in this moment.

Feel the tangible, energetic shift.

As your heart light expands, your ascension column opens. The divine life force energy which anchors you in the present moment to the crystalline core of earth streams up.

It streams up along your ascension column, up into your sacred awakened heart, up into your divine throat, mind's eye ... and now, entering into, opening, and fully activating your crown level vortex, the area at the very top of your head and just above.

Enter into this space by focusing your attention there and allowing light to flow upward as you vibrationally lift with this up-flow of light to expand. Through your crown level of awareness, tune into the divine being you are.

Elevate beyond the experience of lack and judgment, transcending duality to experience the perfect balance within and around you now, to experience your perfect oneness and harmony with Divine, All That Is, Source—with all of creation and with all potential for creation.

Simply bask in divine light and shine forth your divine light to dance, to intermix, to harmonize and come into perfect coherence with the divine soul song which recalibrates your physical body, attuning you to your soul tone, the divine blueprint for your physical expression.

In this moment, your team of guides, guardian angels, and the archangels you are most in resonance with at a soul level and a divine level enter in.

They lift you on wings of love and support you in embodying your highest divine self and truth—embodying the energy of divine blessings, sending forth blessings of love to your surroundings, to the earth, to all beings, to everything exactly as it is right here and now.

Send your blessing of love, harmony, and peace. Tune into the space around your physical body now, allowing the light of your highest divine self to fill this space.

Your divine light and presence expand out beyond you as far as you can imagine ... to the earth level consciousness.

Feel your oneness with the crystalline grid, with galactic level consciousness and with Divine, Source, All That Is, in this place, at this time, amidst the full knowingness of the harmony and perfection and possibility of All That Is, in balance and in vibrational alignment with the knowing that all is well.

Let yourself focus on a potential you would like to create in your life.

Focus on an experience you would like to have, a possibility you would like to manifest, a blessing you would like to see unfold. And let the complete picture of this blessing be painted in the space around you.

Feel, see, experience, and know this specific possibility within the infinite.

What does it look like?

How does your heart respond?

Feel your energy body and your light intermixing with this, your creation, on the inner plane of infinite possibility.

What are you doing inside this creation? What does it open you up to? What potentials exist for this specific creation to serve in the highest interest of all?

Let this be an intention, for what you are calling forth will not only enrich and bring joy into your life experience, but will create ripples of blessing for all beings, that all may harmoniously create in alignment with love, in the highest interest of all.

Let yourself now tune into gratitude for your life experience exactly as it is—for the blessings, the beauty, and the magic of your life.

And now, tune into the gratitude for your inner creation, for your opportunity to co-create with the divine, with your highest light. And now, as you look upon your creation with the eyes of love, see through the illusion to see that it is simply light.

It is simply divine presence, simply energy that has painted this beautiful picture of what you are calling forth, so that when you return your awareness to your physical body in this present point of time, retaining your expanded vibration and your divine perspective, you see the golden light, the rays of divine light, the threads of divine love, the trail of divine light from the perfect expression of your creation on the inner realms into your physical life now.

Allow your heart to open and expand, filling with golden light, which now acts like a magnet for your specific creation within the realm of infinite possibility.

And with your heart shining bright, the trail of divine light—the threads of love, the rays of divine creation—increase in radiance, more tangibly and physically connecting you to your creation you have begun weaving with light on the inner realm.

It is now magnetizing into physical form, into your life, according to divine will, in the highest interest of all.

Imagine yourself magnetizing the golden light of your inner vision to you, so that now, within your physical body, in your physical life, this golden light of your inner creation is all around you. You may experience it first as just light, vibrant, blissful energy surrounding you.

Tune into gratitude for this crystalline divine light you've called forth.

And now, through your open heart and your inner eyes, let yourself see that this light contains the codes for your creation aligned with you in the physical.

And now, let it rise to your awareness. What is a step that you can take now to more fully anchor this manifestation into your life?

Open your heart and receive the knowing of the tangible action you can take. Tune into gratitude for the incredible light all around you and within you.

Imagine now that all of this light of your creation is compressing down now into your heart center, elevating the vibration of your heart light, filling your heart with light, expanding your heart, so that you are embodying it, you are holding it, you are one with it, and it is one with you.

And now, use this light to once again flow forth the blessings of love towards the earth, the blessings of peace and harmony towards humanity, health and vitality and kindness for all beings.

Flow forth the blessings of love and joy, overflowing blessings of love and light.

Receive this love and light to replenish your inner divine being, to more fully and completely embody this divine light in your physical life.

This opens you up to your ability to flow these blessings forth, to freely share your light in a way that does not drain or lower your vibration, but expands your awareness and opens you up to more completely and fully embody all that you are, including manifesting the intention you have set, the creation you have seated, in a way that is in alignment with what you've seen or sown … or even better.

Let your light expand and shine brightly around you in perfect harmony and resonance with love, creating waves of love, ripples of love out beyond you, spanning a distance that is vast, far, and wide, to bring love and light and blessing to all beings, including but not limited to the highest specific potentials of infinite possibility that will most benefit you and your life here and now.

As you, moment by moment and day by day, strive to return to this awareness, remain in love and presence.

Blessings will continue to flow forth from you towards all through your presence. They will continue to weave into your personal experience as blessings flow into your life, bringing you joy and love in the highest interest of all.

Remain open to receiving inspired nudges from your highest divine self, from your guides and angels, your inner divine team, as to the specific steps and actions to take, trusting that you are guided and supported. The more you love and the more you overflow, the more the divine light of infinite possibility can be created and the specific potentials will truly fulfill and excite and reward you and overflow with blessings for all.

This is high-vibrational manifestation.

This is creating in oneness and resonance with your full light and presence as a divine being.

You may wish to simply continue to bask in this openhearted place more deeply while vividly experiencing who you really are and sending out the waves, the blessings, the love vibration, to heal, uplift, honor and simply love all.

We love you.

We bless you as an individual, embodying your highest divine expression and as an essential divine piece, a perfect divine fractal of Source—one with, in harmony with, in perfect coherence with the love that is interwoven, connecting All.

And so, it is.

Thank you, thank you, thank you!

DIAMOND LIGHT ACTIVATION SERIES

Diamond Light is a form of incredibly high vibrational spiritual energy broadcast from the Celestial Realms. Diamond Light is an energetic tool and Gift on this planet from The Council of Light that you can now start to tap into.

When you call in Diamond Light it instantly serves to elevate and harmonize the energies within and around you. Once you tap into the frequency of Diamond Light, the highest Divine Possibilities of the Infinite truly become available to you.

Diamond Light frequency is one of the easiest ways to renew your spirit, so you can enjoy a magical fresh start ... one with infinite opportunities for adding more love, light, & happiness to your life.

That's why I know you're going to love the channeled audio Diamond Light Activation Series with the Council of Light.

The Diamond Light Activation Series consists of 5 high frequency audio recordings that have been channeled with the Archangels and the Council of Light. Each session is designed to help you lift higher and progress further along your divine path by integrating your highest self, and embodying Diamond Light.

These audio sessions are incredibly easy to use ... all you have to do is press "play," listen, and relax. Your angels and The Council of Light will handle all the rest!

Visit:

www.DiamondLightActivations.com

ABOUT THE AUTHOR

Melanie Beckler is an internationally acclaimed best-selling author, angelic channel, and creator of www.Ask-Angels.com. Her books, angel messages, courses and meditations provide a direct link to the love, frequency and wisdom from the angelic and spiritual realms for people around the world.

Melanie's life dramatically changed on January 14, 2008. The lost, confused, and recent college graduate was inspired to begin directly channeling answers from the angelic realm.

"While I had a million other things to focus on, like what I was going to do with my life and how I was going to earn a living, the angels and the realms of spirit completely captured my attention."

Melanie enrolled in psychic development sessions and took professional channeling classes to understand her connection. She spent countless hours meditating and reading to gain a grasp of the metaphysical energies she was experiencing.

Melanie embarked upon a journey of channeling readings and messages from the angels. Four years later, she compiled her first book of channeled angel messages, *Let Your Light Shine.*

Today, Melanie remains focused on publishing the empowering teachings from spirit to assist humanity and earth in the ascension process.

For more information on Melanie's work, visit her website at: **www.Ask-Angels.com**

You can also connect with Melanie on social media:

Facebook: facebook.com/askangelsfan

YouTube: youtube.com/askangels

Twitter: twitter.com/askangels

Instagram: instagram.com/askangels

Pinterest: pinterest.com/askangels

FREE .MP3 ANGEL MESSAGE

To experience an audio Angel Meditation channeled by Melanie, download your FREE .mp3 audio meditation here:

www.ask-angels.com/mp3

ENERGY HEALING WITH YOUR ANGELS

Ready for More?

Get A FREE COPY of "***Energy Healing With Your Angels***" Now!

Visit:

www.ask-angels.com/book

Printed in Great Britain
by Amazon

76227341R00159